Baltic Postcolonial Narratives

Baltic Postcolonial Narratives:

Literature and Power

By

Almantas Samalavičius

**Cambridge
Scholars**
Publishing

Baltic Postcolonial Narratives: Literature and Power

By Almantas Samalavičius

This book first published 2023

Cambridge Scholars Publishing

Lady Stephenson Library, Newcastle upon Tyne, NE6 2PA, UK

British Library Cataloguing in Publication Data
A catalogue record for this book is available from the British Library

ISBN (10): 1-5275-1902-3
ISBN (13): 978-1-5275-1902-2

TABLE OF CONTENTS

FOREWORD

This small book has been in the making for quite some time. In fact, I intended to write a book-length inquiry into Lithuanian prose writing from a postcolonial perspective almost a quarter of a century ago. This was an idea I cherished in a period of intellectual scarcity when some scholars (including myself) realized that Lithuanian literary criticism was badly lacking new and adequate intellectual tools to analyze some interesting and important fictional texts that were then rejected and labeled as popular fiction, or, worse, as mass culture or even pornographic literature. Accordingly, some of Lithuania's best contemporary writers and their writings were either routinely bypassed or otherwise dismissed by literary scholars and critics writing book reviews and essays for daily papers, literary weeklies, and cultural magazines.

Coincidentally, this was also a time full of paradoxes. The literary culture of the first post-Soviet decade could be described in some aspects as booming like never before or, for that matter, any time later. Lithuania's most popular daily papers contained regular book review sections, eagerly published informative overviews of literary developments, and interviewed the leading fiction writers on a regular basis. Writers even appeared on TV talk shows or even the news. Moreover, the leading Lithuanian dailies were competing with each other by launching their literary supplements and hiring well-known authors and/or critics to edit their cultural sections. Fortunately or unfortunately, these days are now over, and the national media these days is not much interested in literature or individuals who write fiction, except on rare occasions when they focus on some best-selling (primarily international) authors or overview large literary events like the annual Vilnius Book Fair.

I started contemplating the first version of this book, focusing on Lithuanian prose writing and its relationship with postcolonialism, after I came back from teaching Lithuanian culture and literature at the University of Illinois at Chicago (UIC) during the Spring 1999 semester. However, after writing a draft of several chapters, I had to give this up for a while as I became involved in other ambitious intellectual projects. These developed into scholarly monographs that were eventually published both in Lithuania and in the USA.

Nevertheless, the idea of writing a book on Lithuanian prose from a postcolonial perspective continued to haunt my imagination. Moreover, two years before I went to Chicago, I was invited to teach a graduate course on Lithuanian contemporary literature and criticism at Vilnius University. At this time, I realized that students had been habitually indoctrinated to dislike and ignore some of the most interesting Lithuanian fiction writers, such as Ričardas Gavelis. This strange discovery revitalized my urge to apply postcolonial theory to Lithuanian (and Baltic) fiction.

The idea of a book eventually took shape in my mind and gradually began to take a more material and organized form. Embracing this self-inflicted writing project, I returned to UIC in the early spring of 2002 as a visiting scholar in the Department of Baltic Languages and Literatures. As I spent a busy few months working on this research project focused on Lithuanian literary postcolonialism, I discovered that Irish scholars were also starting to apply postcolonialism to the study of their literature. This gave me confidence that my own pursuit was well-grounded.

Both stays in Chicago were extremely fruitful and beneficial as I was provisioned with a stimulating intellectual milieu and had (as it then seemed to me) almost unlimited access to the resources of UIC's substantial academic library. Needless to say, library resources, especially in the field of culture and literary theory, were scarce in my home country. During that period, local academic libraries in Lithuania (and elsewhere in Eastern Europe) badly lacked funding and international networking; thus, borrowing the books I needed for my particular purpose was a regular headache.

During the years after my sojourn in Chicago, I drafted some chapters of the book and submitted a book proposal to several national funding agencies. However, to my dismay, the efforts to secure any further funding failed spectacularly. The reasons were quite obvious and not at all surprising; however, this did not provide me with much comfort. Postcolonial theory was then generally viewed as something that had nothing to do with either Eastern European or Baltic social and cultural realities and traditions. In local academia, it was not considered to apply to any serious study of the post-Soviet space. Ironically, the same applied to post-communist studies that were bypassed in Lithuanian academic culture at the time.

Thus, during the first two decades that followed Lithuania's independence and the demise of the Soviet system, the idea of writing a serious academic book on Lithuanian postcolonialism was treated as an eccentric endeavor or, perhaps, even something worse than that. Most older (and institutionally more influential) academic literary scholars viewed such efforts as a subversive revisionist activity.

Unable to secure any funding, I had no other option than to shelve the book in progress. With certain regrets, I chose to redirect my intellectual energy to other ideas that finally developed into a handful of scholarly books on architecture, urbanism, and higher education. At the same time, there were some other shifts in my professional and intellectual career. After almost two decades of writing regular literary criticism and book reviews for daily papers and literary weeklies and monthlies, I gradually retired from these activities. However, I continued to contribute academic essays and articles focused on various literary topics to mostly international books, anthologies, and journals.

Around 2008, in addition to my regular full-time academic duties as a professor at the School of Architecture at Vilnius Gediminas Technical University, I received an invitation to teach postcolonialism, cultural, and media studies at Vilnius University as an adjunct professor. Accepting this generous invitation, I revived my long-term interest in Lithuanian postcolonialism that, in fact, had never disappeared; rather, it had been waiting for the right time to return. My graduate seminars in the Department of English at Vilnius University provided me with an excellent environment in which to rethink some of my early ideas critically while also urging me to return to the previously abandoned book project.

The present academic and intellectual climate both in Lithuania and elsewhere in the Baltic, and, more generally, in Eastern Europe, is far more favorable for the pursuit of postcolonial studies than during the first two post-Soviet decades. As already mentioned, postcolonialism was then viewed with suspicion as an academic subject, and the very few scholars who attempted to analyze local culture through the lens of postcolonial studies felt isolated and marginalized. Luckily, this is no longer the case, and postcolonialism is now embraced more willingly not only by literary scholars but also by Lithuanian (and other Baltic) academics researching theater, film, and/or visual art studies, political science, and even, occasionally, history, a subject that, at least in Lithuania, was and is slow in accepting the postcolonial approach as a fully legitimate form of analytical discourse.

To cut a long story short, the current climate is thus far more favorable for such studies, and the circle of individuals interested in the perspectives of postcolonial studies and their application to Baltic societies and their cultures is slowly yet steadily growing. Current academic and public discussions on themes related to the development of postcolonial approaches to studying post-Soviet societies have become not only more frequent but also more intellectually stimulating, engaging, and inclusive. Luckily, they have also become less confrontational. Last but not least, Baltic scholars have additionally started to critically question the methods and certainties of postcolonial studies rather than reject these studies out of intellectual prejudice. I hope all this will contribute to further considerations of the uses and misuses of postcolonialism, its potential, and, perhaps, its inevitable limits.

In any case, I hope this small book will contribute to these developments in some way by creating a more favorable intellectual atmosphere and enlarging the scope of academic interests while simultaneously providing some insights for further thinking and rethinking the past, present, and future of Baltic societies, their cultures, and their literatures.

ACKNOWLEDGMENTS

I am indebted to several individuals who have, in one way or another, helped me to shape my ideas at different periods of my academic and intellectual career, even before I set out to write this particular book.

Professor Dr. Wolfgang Iser played an important part in shaping my interests in the realms of literary theory, aesthetics, and philosophy that, unbeknownst to him, finally led me to embrace postcolonial studies. My fellowship at the renowned Stuttgart Seminar in Cultural Studies in 1993 and Professor Iser's guiding power encouraged me to maintain and pursue my interests in literary theory even during the somewhat darker periods when this engagement seemingly made little sense. Though, for several reasons, I could not accept Professor Iser's generous invitation to join him as his teaching assistant at the University of California, Irvine, where he was teaching following his retirement from Konstanz University, I will always remain grateful for his intellectual support, goodwill, and mentorship early in my academic career.

My interest in postcolonial studies, which I had already been pursuing for a couple of years, was strengthened significantly by a meeting with Professor David Chioni Moore, who visited Vilnius in the first decade after the fall of the Soviet regime, and I remain grateful for this highly stimulating exchange. I am also indebted to my conversations with Professor Patrick Sheeran, who visited Vilnius University and engaged me in discussions focused on varieties of postcolonialism after reading my essay in *Partisan Review*. These gave me some new insights as well as an awareness that I was pursuing something more real than phantom.

I sincerely thank Professor Violeta Kelertas, with whom I worked on postcolonial Baltic issues in a parallel universe for several decades. I am greatly indebted to her for inviting me to teach at the University of Illinois at Chicago in 1999 and accepting me as a visiting scholar at this institution a few years later. Violeta shared my interest in interpreting Ričardas Gavelis in a postcolonial key and published some of my essays in the journal she was then editing, and she urged me to contribute to her groundbreaking volume *Baltic Postcolonialism*.

My thanks are also due to Professor Regina Rudaitytė, who was *a spiritus movens* responsible for involving me with the English Department at Vilnius University, where I have been teaching graduate seminars for the last fifteen years in addition to my primary duties at the School of Architecture at Vilnius Gediminas Technical University. The series of international conferences Regina organized at Vilnius University was exceptional in bringing together highly interesting and leading academics from different parts of Europe and the UK and provoking valuable and memorable intellectual discussions. I also thank Dr. Antanas Smetona, the former dean of the Faculty of Philology at Vilnius University, who was always supportive.

Finally, a brief note on the text of the present book. Though I have published academic articles on various aspects of Lithuanian postcolonialism in international journals and anthologies over the years, I opted not to include them in this book as I believe they are already in suitable contexts. However, I would like to thank the quarterly journal *Lituanus* for their permission to include "Revisiting Postcolonial Studies and the Baltics" (first published in *Lituanus* 69, no. 1, pp. 27–41) in this book in a slightly different and extended version as well as to reproduce my article "Beyond the Enigma of Power: Notes On The Last Novel by Ričardas Gavelis" (first published in *Lituanus* 65, no. 3, pp. 38–49).

INTRODUCTION

POSTCOLONIALISM TAKES COMMAND

During recent decades, a new field of research known as postcolonial theory, or more often (and possibly more accurately) as postcolonial studies, has gained currency in the shifting landscape of the humanities. After emerging during the 1970s and undergoing a rapid development and experiencing numerous re-adjustments, postcolonialism has finally established its academic and scholarly reputation, especially during the last three decades, and it has made its way into the teaching programs and research projects of many Western and non-Western universities alike. It was during this period that postcolonial studies acquired a global character as well as international academic support, becoming a booming and yet inexhaustible academic industry all over the globe. Postcolonial theorists and critics have raised a number of important theoretical and political issues and mapped out new trajectories for postcolonial critique and cultural analysis. Quite naturally, Europe and the West, as well as their discourses, have become the legitimate targets of postcolonial critique. Bearing in mind that it was European powers that engaged in colonizing the rest of the world after Columbus 'discovered' America, this focus is reasonable and understandable. However, this persistent focus curiously obscures the colonial activities of non-European or quasi-European powers. For example, the *Encyclopedia Britannica*'s entry on postcolonialism focuses exclusively on European and Western colonialism and emphasizes the European legacy rather than considering any other versions of colonialism and imperialism.

Postcolonial theorists and historians have been concerned with investigating the various trajectories of modernity as understood and experienced from a range of philosophical, cultural, and historical perspectives. They have been particularly concerned with engaging with the ambiguous legacy of the Enlightenment—as expressed in social, political, economic, scientific, legal, and cultural thought—beyond Europe itself. The legacy is ambiguous, according to postcolonial theorists, because the age of Enlightenment was also an age of empire, and the connection between those two historical epochs is more than incidental.[1]

One of the features of this field of research and academic studies is its constant and ongoing search for identity, which led to the remapping of its territory and the marking of a lot of new targets. Drawing on various methodologies (Marxism, feminism, post-structuralism, etc.), postcolonial theorists have frequently crossed the usual disciplinary boundaries and ventured into territories beyond literary studies while embracing history, social psychology, anthropology, cultural studies, and the like.

The relatively high fluidity and openness of this field of research and approach was often criticized by older and thus more 'legitimate' academic disciplines; however, in the long run, its broad framework not only contributed to its growth as an academic enterprise but also brought a spectacular expansion of postcolonialism in geographical terms. As Edward Said emphasized quite early in the history of postcolonialism when the methods of postcolonial critique were being shaped: "the main strengths of postcolonial analysis is that it widens, instead of narrows, the interpretive perspective, which is another way of saying that it liberates instead of further constricting and colonising the mind."[2] The liberating force of postcolonial studies is now being witnessed in various geographic localities. They provide a powerful and more than adequate tool for intellectuals and academics of 'Third World' countries and inform researchers trying to understand Western colonialism from the inside. Besides, since the demise of the communist system and the so-called Second World, scholars in this 'gray' domain have set their eyes on postcolonial studies and attempted to unlock their potential for studying their own societies.

As postcolonial studies progressed, there were numerous attempts to provide a solid ground for further inquiry into political, social, and cultural issues related to a domain formerly described as the Third World. Thus, many assumptions were questioned, theoretical positions and attitudes were debated and even negated, and the possibilities of introducing a new paradigm of analyzing the colonial legacy and the realities of the postcolonial world were researched. Consequently, the boundaries of what could be considered colonial or postcolonial were constantly drawn and re-drawn. The editors of *The Empire Writes Back*, a highly influential collective work on postcolonialism, went as far as describing almost each and every country that was, in one way or another, subjected to colonialism as postcolonial. According to them:

> [T]he literatures of African countries, Australia, Bangladesh, Canada, Caribbean countries, India, Malaysia, Malta, New Zealand, Pakistan, Singapore, South Pacific Island countries, and Sri Lanka are all postcolonial literatures. The literature of the USA should also be placed in this category. Perhaps because of its current position of power, and the neo-colonizing role

it has played, its post-colonial nature has not been generally recognized. But its relationship with the metropolitan centre as it evolved over the last two centuries has been paradigmatic for postcolonial literatures everywhere. What each of these literatures has in common beyond their special and distinctive regional characteristics is that they emerged in their present form out of the experience of colonization and asserted themselves by foregrounding the tension with the imperial power, and by emphasizing their differences from the assumptions of the imperial centre. It is this which makes them distinctly postcolonial.[3]

This list of societies labeled as postcolonial is, of course, incomplete, even in terms of English-speaking countries, not to mention the specific and often significant differences making these countries and societies difficult objects for comparison. Some scholars viewed these early attempts as questionable and highly problematic. As the interest in analyzing experiences of colonialism progressed, more and more authors realized that despite containing certain common features, the phenomenon of colonialism was far more complex than the authors of the above-mentioned anthology suggested. As Marion O'Callaghan emphasized while rethinking postcolonialism: "It varied over periods, it differed in the ways it operated, it differed in the ways political independence was achieved, granted or withheld."[4] Thus, understanding the complexities of colonialism and analyzing the different forms it took enabled postcolonial scholars to expand the boundaries of this phenomenon in order to outline its common features and the specific character of any of its forms. Eventually, a broad interpretation of colonialism and postcoloniality came into being. However, as Ela Shohat, for example, insisted, such a broad understanding of postcoloniality came with a price. As she insightfully remarked,

This problematic formulation collapses very different national-racial formations—the United States, Australia, and Canada, on the one hand, and Nigeria, Jamaica, and India, on the other—as equally "postcolonial." Positioning Australia and India in relation to an imperial center simply because they were both colonies, for example, equates the relations of the colonized white settlers to the Europeans at the center with that of the colonized indigenous populations to the Europeans. It also assumes that white settler states and emerging Third World nations broke away from the "center" in the same way. Similarly, white Australians and aboriginal Australians are placed on the same "periphery," as though they were cohabitants vis-à-vis the "center." The critical differences between Europe's genocidal oppression of Aborigines in Australia, indigenous peoples of the Americas, and Afro-diasporic communities, *and* Europe's domination of European elites in the colonies are leveled with an easy stroke of the "post." The term "postcolonial" in this sense masks the white settlers' colonialist-racist policies toward indigenous peoples not only before independence but also after the official break from the imperial center, while also de-emphasizing neocolonial global positionings of First World settler states.[5]

This criticism of the term 'postcolonial' is well-known and was the subject of numerous discussions inside and outside the communities of postcolonial scholars. Looking back at these discussions with a certain temporal distance (and a different geographical location), Shohat's criticism of how the authors of *The Empire Writes Back* perceived the notion of postcoloniality can be considered in many ways accurate and just. However, it also contained certain contradictions as this kind of revisionism could effectively cause other scholars to avoid any generalizations of the term or reduce it to some very few cultures and societies, what is known today as 'classical colonialism.'

To a certain extent, Shohat's insistence on the limits of the term 'postcolonial' has played an ambiguous role in further inquiries into the conceptualization of postcolonialism as it encouraged researchers to concentrate on the specific experience of non-white and aboriginal communities in some countries colonized and dominated by the European powers and, at the same time, narrowed the applicability of the term. Thus, good intentions do not always produce the desired result but rather provide new grounds for new contradictions and ambiguities that are – and hopefully will continue to be – revisited, scrutinized, and contested.

It is no wonder that postcolonial theory has been criticized from both outside and inside the field. As Leela Gandhi recently observed while reviewing developments in this field,

> While postcolonial theorists have attempted variously to defend the politics of their academic practice, recent critics of postcolonial theorizing have asserted the unsustainable distance between the self-reflexive preoccupations of the post-colonial academy, on the one hand, and the concerns arising from, and relevant to, postcolonial realities, on the other.
>
> Some vigilant and self-critical postcolonial theorists agree that the academic labour of postcolonialism is often blind to its own socially deleterious effect. Among this group, Gayatri Spivak is salutary in her warning that recent concessions to marginality studies within the first-world metropolitan academy inadvertently serve to identify, confirm, and thereby exclude certain cultural formations as chronically marginal. The celebratory 'third worldism' of postcolonial studies, Spivak cautions, may well perpetuate real social and political oppressions which rely upon rigid distinctions between the 'centre' and the 'margin.'[6]

However, despite all the confusions and contradictions related to the problematic nature and character of postcolonialism, it can be concluded that the term can hardly be understood as mono-functional. Thus, it means different things in different contexts as well as in geographical, historical, and cultural realms.

Attempts have been made to distinguish between the two stages embedded in postcolonialism: a colonial period (or phase) during which the colonizers dominated, suppressing the culture, history, and memory of colonized people and imposing their institutions, and a postcolonial (post-independence) period during which the internalization of colonizers' values are questioned and examined and the trauma of colonization is acknowledged. However, as Alfred J. Lopez has emphasized, the latter phase is far more complex as "the colonized culture's previous complicities with the colonizer – and present acceptance and internalization of the colonizer's cultural values and knowledge – come to light and are, again less successfully, suppressed."[7]

This period, which starts with regaining independence, is especially complicated and often lengthy, with no clearly foreseeable and/or forecastable end. It is also marked by internal contradictions as the values and experiences of different generations collide, memories of the past differ widely, and political and cultural ambitions conflict with realities and policies. This intermediate period is frequently described as decolonization, yet other categories like postcolonialism or postcoloniality are often applied instead, avoiding political implications inherent to (political) decolonization.

Nevertheless, some authors have insisted on the importance of decolonization, not only as a legitimate goal and practice of postcolonial political and social transformation but also as a practice related to the cultural and literary imagination. Jan Nederveen Pieterse and Bhikhu Parekh have argued that

> Since colonization was a highly complex process, decolonization lacks a clear focus and target. It may be easy to resent and attack foreign rulers or capital, but it is extremely difficult to identify what values, institutions and identities are foreign and part of colonial legacy. And if one succeeds in identifying some of them, they are sometimes too deeply intertwined with their endogenous analogues to be clearly separated from them. Even if one manages to isolate some of them, one is sometimes so deeply shaped and moulded by them as to be unable to reject them without rejecting parts of oneself. Even as colonialism did not involve the imposition of something entirely foreign, decolonization cannot consist in discarding what is deemed to be alien. Colonialism evolved a new consciousness out of a subtle mixture of the old and new; decolonization has to follow the same route. It requires not only the restoration of a historically continuous and allegedly pure

precolonial heritage, but an imaginative creation of a new form of consciousness and way of life.[8]

Though some critics are inclined to dismiss suggestions of the continuity of decolonization and refuse to admit the open-endedness of this long-term and complex process in the same way as some social scientists have claimed that the transitory post-communist period terminated as soon as post-Soviet Eastern European societies joined the European Union, this kind of optimistic attitude poses inevitable risks. First and foremost, it can simplify a complex process and give way to a highly questionable linear perspective of looking at the past or, for that matter, the present. Moreover, we have already experienced the naïve and premature predictions of the 'end of history,' once glibly proposed by Francis Fukuyama, or even earlier concerns about 'the end of ideology.' Despite these premature claims, we have witnessed the end of neither history nor ideology. On the contrary, versions of history have proliferated in the same way as ideologies have multiplied.

Thus, when approaching such highly complex and closely intertwined issues as decolonization or postcoloniality, it is advisable to refrain from any hasty and ill-founded preliminary predictions because, as Leela Gandhi has rightly argued, "whenever postcolonialism identifies itself with the epochal 'end' of colonialism, it become falsely utopian or prematurely celebratory."[9] So far, proponents of these 'end of' concepts have not become eye-witnesses of the fulfillment of these grandiose prophecies.

Perhaps the same precaution applies to the geographical limits of postcolonialism. Though it is only natural that the emergence of postcolonial discourse was intricately related to the dismantling of colonial regimes after World War II and the socio-political processes that followed, these transitions have largely demonstrated the problematic nature as well as enormous complexity of postcolonial developments, not to mention the array of internal issues inherent to postcolonial theorizing that gradually matured, acquiring more introspection, self-reflection, and conscious and subconscious self-criticism.

Together with the conceptualization of related intellectual tools and categories, such as center-periphery, dependency, mimicry, hybridity, otherness, etc., postcolonial discourse has expanded beyond its original premises and limits of consciousness. The geographical expansion of postcolonialism is also instructive. The successor to what has previously been understood as the Third World, postcolonialism has since embraced some of the territories previously attributed to the (now extinct) Second World and even the First World itself.

The spectacular development of Irish postcolonialism is perhaps the most telling transformation of postcolonial critique. The relatively late arrival of Irish postcolonial studies demonstrated that there were curious cases of Europe or the West practicing no more and no less than the colonization of itself when such European superpowers as England subjugated and dominated its closest neighboring country for a number of centuries. However, the road of Irish studies toward a postcolonial perspective has not been easy. This has been noted by various Irish scholars, who have discussed the factors that prevented the formation of Irish postcolonial studies for a long time. A couple of decades ago, C. L. Innes questioned the state of the art as well as the prospects for Irish studies when encountering postcolonialism:

> Does the inclusion of Ireland lead one to modify our thinking about the nature of colonial and postcolonial relationships, histories and cultures? And why have discussions of the 'postcolonial' made relatively little relevance to Ireland? Although Irish literary critics have begun to invoke Said, Fanon and others, and to see them as providing a useful perspective from which to view the relationship between Irish and British cultural history, the major theorists in the postcolonial arena have generally ignored Ireland.[10]

Since this evaluation was given in 2000, many things have changed. As early as 1998, there were scholars who acknowledged the undeniable importance of a postcolonial attitude to the study of Irish literature, arguing that 'colonialism' remains a valid and promising category while studying Irish culture and literature.[11] The reluctance that persisted for some time finally gave way to rethinking the framework of postcolonial studies. Since then, there has been significant progress in Irish studies toward using and accepting the postcolonial agenda and shaping its own tools of inquiry. Despite initially being met with skepticism and ignorance, Irish postcolonial studies gradually expanded their focus on the postcolonial perspective. By now, a significant amount of important scholarly work has been produced in this field, contributing to the awareness of the multifaced nature of this process.[12] As Eoin Flannery remarked in his introduction to the issue of *Postcolonial Text* devoted to Irish postcolonialism,

> The impact of theory, or specifically the advent of an Irish franchise of postcolonial studies, has produced a contentious, as well as progressive, commerce of ideas and theoretical paradigms within the broader discourse of Irish studies. Despite the poststructuralist murkiness, paradigmatic vanity, and indulgent verbosity of some international postcolonial theory, the resources of postcolonial literary theory and historiography provide singly-enabling mechanisms for Irish cultural inquiry. Indeed such critical importation

became, and remains, what might be nominated a postcolonial cathexis
within Irish studies. [...] Postcolonial studies is manifestly concerned with
foregrounding exigent historical and contemporary experiences and legacies
of all forms of imperialism. By facilitating discussions of imperial and anti-
imperial experience across borders and within a protracted historical
continuum, theoretical readings strive to, indeed must contribute to, ethical
readings of colonialism, neo-colonialism, and postcolonialism.[13]

Irish studies was not the only field that embraced postcolonialism after
realizing its potential to analyze various aspects of society and culture
colonized and dominated by a foreign power. The collapse of the Soviet
Union and the re-establishment of independence in Lithuania, Latvia, and
Estonia – the three countries colonized by the USSR in 1940 (and, much
earlier, by Imperial Russia) – as well as the emerging post-Soviet space in
Eastern Europe and processes of political liberation in areas of Central Asia
formerly dominated by Moscow were all soon subjects for post-communist
studies. When scholars in Eastern Europe and those studying the regional
transformations in North America sought a new theoretical basis for
sociocultural and political analysis, postcolonialism seemed to offer
prospective intellectual tools and research agenda. Of course, the uncritical
application of postcolonialism to Eastern Europe had its own risks. Thus,
researchers of the post-communist space faced a challenge – how to apply
the categories and conceptualizations of postcolonialism to local studies
while getting rid of the excessive dominance of ideological mono-culture
that had dominated social analysis in the post-war era until the fall of the
Iron Curtain.

Students of Eastern Europe adopting postcolonial methods were initially
not greeted particularly warmly, to say the least – and sometimes with
considerable caution, skepticism, and even open hostility by scholars
practicing postcolonial studies in the West. This undisguised distrust and
hostility was also related to other differences between Western and East
European scholars. After the collapse of the communist system, the
asymmetry between Eastern European and Western scholarship focusing on
the region was clearly visible. Local scholars in Eastern Europe lacked
adequate institutional infrastructure, substantial funding resources, and
timely support from state research policies. The relationships and forms of
cooperation between the privileged scholars from North America and their
'junior brothers and sisters' in Eastern Europe were not always successful
and often lacked mutual understanding, sometimes leading to unequal
competition or even new forms of dominance – especially in the powerful
dominance of Western discourse.

During the first decade after the fall of the Iron Curtain, post-communist studies were supposed to replace the compromised (and largely vulgarised) Marxist ideology that dominated during the period of communism. Accordingly, as in the case of Irish studies, postcolonialism in Baltic societies was considered not to fit the agenda of post-communist studies. Likewise,[14] racial categories in the Baltic milieu and context were considered as 'given' without attempting to rethink their emergence and boundaries or to view them as social constructs that were socially engineered at a certain time. Few attempts (if any) were made to analyze how the regimes of Tsarist Russia and, later, the Soviet Union treated people from the societies they conquered and exploited.

It is, nevertheless, well-known that despite its critical discourse about colonialism, fascism, and other 'Western-generated' ideologies, the Soviet Union pursued a policy of colonization in its immediate neighborhood. Accordingly, its non-Russian population was viewed as inferior in many aspects. People from the colonized lands (the Baltic and Central Asia) were never treated as equals. Though all nations and ethnic groups were officially declared equal under Soviet legislation, the reality was very different. This inferiority of other nations and ethnic communities is evidenced by the fact that the Moscow authorities never trusted even the most subservient communists in the colonized countries that became Soviet 'republics.' The position of the 'second secretary' of the Communist Party in each and every republic was meant to be filled by a Russian, who was selected and appointed to this post by Moscow. In fact, these 'second' secretaries had more power than the first secretary, traditionally elected from among local nationals and whose status was reminiscent of the one enjoyed by governors-general during Russia's imperial era.

These inevitable collisions between scholars attempting to study the Baltic societies through the lens of postcolonial theory and postcolonial theorists who embraced Marxism and fell into the orthodoxy of racial categorization and the lack of common language had their own impact on the development and quality of post-Soviet studies. For a long period, these differences in ideological attitudes and the identification of scholarly communities preserved mental and institutional barriers that excluded the post-Soviet space from the 'legitimate' interest of postcolonial studies.

Although most of the institutional barriers have been dismantled more or less successfully over several decades, some of the mental barriers still exist. However, today, the conceptualization of postcolonialism and its application to the post-Soviet space are no longer considered eccentric activities but are gradually becoming more or less routine research activities that challenge and overcome established difficulties. A growing awareness of the complexity of postcolonial studies and ongoing examinations of the development of postcolonial discourse have resulted in its potential as well as its limitations being realized. The initial enthusiasm of some early postcolonial critics of the Baltic cultures has also now become more self-reflective and self-critical.

Instead of submitting uncritically to the agenda of postcolonial studies, local scholars are trying to sort out which concepts and research strategies can and cannot be applied to the history and present realities of Baltic societies. In this sense, the awareness of local postcolonial critiques is undergoing significant changes. At the same time, Baltic postcolonial scholars have freed themselves from the image of 'exoticism' inflicted upon them during the early years of the post-Soviet era. Today, I believe more scholars than ever would agree with the observation of Arif Dirlik, who claimed that "'Postcoloniality' represents a response to a genuine need: the need to overcome a crisis of understanding produced by the inability of old categories to account for the world."[15] Some of the challenges of postcolonialism for Baltic scholarship and Eastern European studies are examined in the next chapter.

Notes

[1] *Britannica*, s.v. "postcolonialism," accessed January 14, 2023, https://www.britannica.com/topic/postcolonialism.
[2] Said, "Afterword," 177–185.
[3] Ashcroft et al., eds., *The Empire Writes Back*, 2.
[4] O'Callaghan, "Continuities in Imagination," 22.
[5] Shohat, "Notes on the Post-Colonial," 131–132.
[6] Gandhi, "Postcolonial Theory," 55.
[7] Lopez, "Post and Pasts," 86.
[8] Nederveen Pieterse and Parekh, "Shifting Imaginaries," 3.
[9] Gandhi, "Postcolonial Theory," 174.
[10] Innes, "Postcolonial Studies and Ireland," 21.
[11] Smith, *Decolonization and Criticism*, 35.
[12] On Irish postcolonialism, see Lloyd, *Anomalous States*; Hooper and Graham, eds., *Irish and Postcolonial Theory*; Carroll and King, *Ireland and Postcolonial Theory*; Flannery, *Ireland and Postcolonial Studies*; Davis, *Music, Postcolonialism, and Gender*; Pine, *The Disappointed Bridge*, etc.
[13] Flannery, "Irish Cultural Studies and Postcolonial Theory," 1.
[14] Innes, "Postcolonial Studies and Ireland," 30.
[15] Dirlik, *Postcolonial Aura*, 73.

Works Cited

Ashcroft, Bill, Gareth Griffiths, and Helen Tiffin, eds. *The Empire Writes Back: Theory and Practice in Post-Colonial Literatures*. London: Routledge, 1989.

Britannica, s.v. "Postcolonialism." Accessed January 14, 2023. https://www.britannica.com/topic/postcolonialism.

Carroll, Clare, and Patricia King. *Ireland and Postcolonial Theory*. Notre Dame, IN: Notre Dame University Press, 2003.

Davis, Leith. *Music, Postcolonialism, and Gender: The Construction of Irish National Identity, 1724–1874*. Notre Dame, IN: University of Notre Dame Press, 2005.

Dirlik, Arif. *Postcolonial Aura: Third World Criticism in the Age of Global Capitalism*. Boulder, CO: Westview Press, 1998.

Flannery, Eoin. "Irish Cultural Studies and Postcolonial Theory." *Postcolonial Text* 3, no. 3 (2007): 1–13.

—. *Ireland and Postcolonial Studies: Theory, Discourse, Utopia*. London: Palgrave Macmillan, 2009.

Gandhi, Leela. *Postcolonial Theory: A Critical Introduction*. New York: Columbia University Press, 2019.

Hooper, Glen, and Colin Graham, eds. *Irish and Postcolonial Writing: History, Theory, Practice*. London: Palgrave Macmillan, 2002.

Innes, C. L. "Postcolonial Studies and Ireland." In *Comparing Postcolonial Literatures: Dislocations*, edited by Ashok Berry and Patricia Murray, 21–30. London: Macmillan, 2000.

Lloyd, David. *Anomalous States: Irish Writing and the Post-Colonial Moment*. Durham, NC: Duke University Press, 1993.

Lopez, Alfred A. *Posts and Pasts: A Theory of Postcolonialism*. New York: State University of New York Press, 2001.

Nederveen Pieterse, Jan, and Bhikhu Parekh. "Shifting Imaginaries: Decolonisation, Internal Decolonization, Postcoloniality." In *The Decolonization of Imagination: Culture, Knowledge and Power*, edited by Jan Nederveen Pieterse and Bhikhu Parekh, 1–20. London: Zed Books, 1995.

O'Callaghan, Marion. "Continuities in Imagination." In *The Decolonization of Imagination: Culture, Knowledge and Power*, edited by Jan Nederveen Pieterse and Bhikhu Parekh, 22–42. London: Zed Books, 1995.

Pine, Richard, *The Disappointed Bridge: Ireland and the Post-Colonial World*. Newcastle upon Tyne: Cambridge Scholars Publishing, 2014.

Said, Edward. "Afterword: Reflections on Ireland and Postcolonialism." In *Ireland and Postcolonial Theory*, edited by Clare Carroll and Patricia King, 177–186. Notre Dame, IN: Notre Dame University Press, 2003.

Shohat, Ella. "Notes on the 'Post-Colonial'." In *The Pre-Occupation of Postcolonial Studies*, edited by Fawzia Afzal-Khan and Kalpana Seshadri-Crooks, 126–139. Durham, NC: Duke University Press, 2000.

Smith, Gerry. *Decolonization and Criticism: The Construction of Irish Literature*. London: Pluto Press, 1998.

CHAPTER I

BALTIC POSTCOLONIALISM
AND ITS DISCONTENTS

It is well-known that in the early stage of its development, the concept of postcolonialism was primarily applied to 'classical' or 'historical' colonies, i.e., African or Asian countries and lands colonized by mostly European (super)powers in one historical period or another. As soon as these studies evolved, however, some scholars interested in colonialism and its cultural, political, and social effects soon became dissatisfied with the prevalent understanding and especially the 'geography' of colonialism and postcolonialism. They set out to question the early certainties of this research field and offered views that contained well-grounded criticism concerning ambiguities in (post)colonial discourse.

Edward W. Said was one of the first scholars in the Western hemisphere who realized that colonialism could not be contained within the then-reigning paradigm, which limited this discourse exclusively to African and Asian conquests by the European powers. Being an insightful scholar and an extremely nuanced cultural and literary critic, Said observed that there were non-European powers that were equally as colonialist as their Western counterparts. He realized that one such non-European or semi-European political entity was Imperial Russia, which was and remained a colonial enterprise to no less a degree than the Western European powers that sought to colonize Africa, Asia, and Latin America. Its involvement in colonial activities in the Caucasus, Central Asia, and large parts of Eastern Europe made Russia a colonial power *par excellence* despite the fact that it never went so far as to gain lands in other continents or far-away territories. Instead of reaching into other geographical realms, Russia focused on its immediate neighbors. As Said noted in his influential and highly acclaimed book *Culture and Imperialism*, colonialism was not purely and exclusively a European activity, and he went on to emphasize that

> there are several empires that I do not discuss: the Austro-Hungarian, the Russian, the Ottoman, and the Spanish and Portuguese. These omissions, however, are not at all meant to suggest that Russia's domination of Central

> Asia and Eastern Europe, Istanbul's rule over the Arab world, Portugal's over what are today's Angola and Mozambique, and Spain's domination in both the Pacific and Latin America have been either benign (and hence approved of) or any less imperialist.[1]

Even if he did not explicitly analyze the character and effects of Ottoman or Russian colonization and chose other targets than Imperial Russia, Said nevertheless made an acute remark on Imperial Russia that has a lasting importance for all students of (post)colonialism in suggesting that Russia, under the rule of its tsars,

> acquired its imperial territories almost exclusively by adjacence. Unlike Britain or France, which jumped thousands of miles beyond their own borders to other continents, Russia moved to swallow whatever land or peoples stood next to its borders, which in the process kept moving further and further east and south.[2]

Despite these timely and largely accurate observations, Said's voice remained lonely for at least a couple of decades. Few pioneers in the newly emerging field of postcolonial studies were eager to respond to his challenge and engage in redrawing the field's borders and reconsidering the most widespread notions of (post)colonialism and imperialism.

Occasionally, there were opinions among postcolonial researchers that supported and extended Said's insights. For example, while researching decolonization issues, Muriel E. Chamberlain adroitly noticed that during the Soviet period, Russians had a significant "ethnic, cultural as well as political impact upon Soviet republics." Moreover, she drew attention to the fact that this was a conscious and deliberate policy directed at some of them, especially the Baltic states, that was consolidated and strengthened by relocating their inhabitants to other parts of the Soviet Union.[3] In fact, during the post-war deportations, a lot of Lithuanians, Latvians, and Estonians were deported to Siberia and other parts of the Soviet Union, where many perished because of the unbearable living conditions.

Other early postcolonial scholars, however, were far more interested in the forms of 'classical' colonialism than engaging in uncertain, turbulent, and risky debates about any other interpretative versions of the colonial enterprise, especially those that were hardly seen as legitimate from the viewpoint of postcolonial studies during that early period. Accordingly, the colonialist policies of imperial powers such as Russia and the Soviet Union (or, for that matter, other non-European powers) safely escaped any further scrutiny. Meanwhile, concerns about the applicability of postcolonial studies to the analysis of the post-Soviet and post-communist realm were growing. Scholars of Baltic descent residing in the USA and Canada, as well as younger researchers living in the post-communist realm, were setting their eyes on postcolonial theory as a possible (and promising) intellectual tool for scrutinizing the legacy of Soviet domination over Eastern Europe. Immediately after the fall of the Soviet Union, some scholars in the Baltic states and other Eastern European countries started to search for a new methodological framework for analyzing their societies, as the available intellectual tools were seen as inadequate. One of these new intellectual agendas that offered a fresh perspective for serious scholarly inquiry was postcolonialism.

The American literary scholar David Chioni Moore was one of the first internationally renowned authors who voiced the need to broaden the scope of postcolonial studies to embrace many other nations, but he remained reluctant to incorporate the post-Soviet realm. He argued for applying the postcolonial approach to post-Soviet cultures, emphasizing their diversity and differences, and that, in this sense, these studies' geographic expansion would correspond to the diversity that existed in the postcolonial realm. It was suggested that "the term 'postcolonial,' and everything that goes with it – language, economy, politics, resistance, liberation and its hangover – might reasonably be applied to the formerly Russo- and Soviet-controlled regions post-1989 and -1991, just as it has been applied to South Asia post-1947 or Africa post-1958."[4] However, Moore observed certain obstacles that prevented post-Soviet societies from being approached from the perspective of postcolonial studies, and he set out to explain this strange inadequacy.

> In view of these postcolonial/post-Soviet parallels, two silences are striking. The first is the silence of western postcolonial studies today on the subject of the former Soviet sphere. And the second, mirrored silence is the failure of many scholars (other than those appearing in this volume) specializing in the formerly Soviet-controlled lands to think of their region in the useful postcolonial terms developed by scholars of, say, Indonesia and Gibon. South does not speak east, and east not South. In detailing these two silences, let me turn first to Western postcolonial studies. In notable synoptic articles on postcolonial studies and in recent major classroom-use anthologies (such as those by Williams and Christman, or by Ashcroft et al.), the broadest range of nations is generally mentioned, both colonial and colonized, except for those of the former Soviet sphere. Ella Shohat's fine 1992 article "Notes on the Post-Colonial" – which today is a classical postcolonial-studies-reference – is an excellent example of this silence on the post-Soviet.[5]

His attempts to relocate postcolonialism to the post-Soviet space were not only timely but also played an important part in encouraging Baltic scholars

to apply this theoretical framework to the study of their cultures and
literatures. Unlike some of his colleagues born in the Baltic states before
making their way to the US, Canada, or other countries, Moore was seen as
primarily an American scholar and thus considered less biased than his
colleagues embedded in their Baltic genealogies and consequently not fully
reliable. It might be added that émigré scholars who found themselves in
the US and other parts of the Western world as fugitives of World War II
were treated with a certain distrust by their peers, who occasionally
suspected that they were somewhat biased in their judgments toward the
USSR. Luckily, this was not the case with Moore and his insights. Moore's
thought-provoking article, published in the influential journal *Proceedings
of the Modern Language Association*, contributed to paving the way for
Baltic postcolonialism. However, it took quite a long time for Baltic
postcolonialism to define and defend its territory in the broader field of
postcolonial studies and theory.

Postcolonial Studies and the Post-Communist/ Post-Socialist/Post-Soviet Space

As I have already emphasized, postcolonial studies continued to be rather
reluctant to embrace Eastern European societies and, more generally, the
post-Soviet space for quite a long time for various reasons. During the three
decades after the fall of the Berlin Wall, German unification, the re-
establishment of independence in Lithuania and then its close neighbors
Latvia and Estonia, and, eventually, the dissolution of the USSR, Eastern
Europe as well as other geographical regions that were formerly colonized
and dominated by the Soviet regime underwent complex, complicated, often
quite painful, yet unavoidable epochal transformations. Many things
occurred during these significant socio-political shifts. However, as this
book is focused on the region's literary discourse rather than societal
transformations, I do not intend to take an inventory of the social changes.

Nevertheless, a number of authors have emphasized and outlined the
parallels between the postcolonial and post-socialist/post-communist
conditions. The anthropologist Catherine Verdery was one of the first
scholars in her field to insist on the importance and validity of these
correspondences. She believed that the agenda and methods of postcolonial
studies could be used appropriately in the study of post-socialist societies
and their cultural contexts because dichotomies between the self and the
other – being key categories in postcolonial discourse and applied to the
realities of the Third World – could be located in the Second World, where
they survived as dichotomies of East versus West in the post-socialist

space.[6] Moreover, she saw considerable prospects for the post-Soviet space to be applied to post-Cold War studies, thus being able to integrate and bridge postcolonialism and post-socialism.[7]

There were, of course, more authors who claimed that postcolonial studies could be meaningfully applied to historical and cultural studies of Eastern Europe – especially to countries like Poland that fell prey to the colonial power of Imperial Russia and were eventually taken over by Soviet communism after World War II. Janusz Korek – a founding editor of the online journal *Postcolonial Europe* who insisted on the applicability of postcolonialism to the Eastern and Central European domain – argued that there was an inherent bias in postcolonial studies that caused Central Europe to be ignored in postcolonial debates. This discourse originated during the Cold War era and was developed by scholars on the Left who were associated with Marxism. Furthermore, countries like Poland, in different parts of their history, were first colonizers and then colonized; thus, their status in the eyes of postcolonial scholars was at least ambiguous.[8] Researchers continued to disagree as to whether Eastern and Central Europe, as well as some former republics of the Soviet Union, could be described as truly postcolonial societies.

There was consensus regarding the republics of Central Asia – it was eventually agreed that several Islamic countries were colonized first by Tsarist Russia and then by the Soviet Union – yet debates on Eastern and Central Europe divided postcolonial scholars into supporters and opponents as to their (post)colonial status. In a lengthy article published in *East European Politics and Societies*, Henry F. Carey and Rafal Raciborski provided a well-argued opinion that the post-socialist countries of Eastern and Central Europe were suitable candidates for the status of postcolonial societies. According to them, Russian and Soviet colonialism took a different form to other colonial regimes:

> While Lenin may have obfuscated the distinction between imperialism and colonialism, we can assert that imperialism is a global system of domination that does not necessarily require colonies (the United States being a case in point). Many colonial empires were not global and are imperial under this rubric. Even the Soviet Empire was not imperial, according to this view, because it was too weak to penetrate foreign economies, despite its world-wide aspirations. Colonialism is the more narrow system of domination, based on acquisition of territory in a colony. While we are apt to associate a colony with the overseas territories of the British and the French, the second largest empire, the Russian/Soviet Empire had colonies around its periphery and within it. It could be argued that its western borderlands did not constitute colonies because of their common Orthodox Christian civilization and the small numbers of Russians exported to maintain control. However,

these colonies had the colonial characteristic of local administration subordinated to the metropolitan power, as well as constant resistance to Russian control. Orthodox Christian Romania and Bulgaria were subdued by Soviet troops and, despite their common civilizations with Russia, were semicolonized through communist measures.[9]

Harvard sociologist Laura L. Adams has further argued that despite the lack of general agreement on the character of the Soviet Union as an empire and colonial power, certain parallels between the colonial powers and the Soviet Union can be drawn. Focusing on Central Eurasia, Soviet modernity, its notion of progress, the hierarchy of cultural differences privileging Russian superiority, and the creation of national elites, she emphasized that this region might fall into the category of (post)colonial. Adams concluded her insights by suggesting that,

> In short, the Soviet Union was like an empire in that it crafted political domination over a geographically diverse territory and it imposed a hierarchical culture (with Moscow at its center) over its ethnically diverse citizens. But the Soviet Union was unlike other European empires in a number of ways, the most significant of which was its emphasis on the modernization and political mobilization of the periphery. In this, the Soviet state was much more aggressive than other colonial powers in its attack on the inner, spiritual realm that Central Asians sought to defend.[10]

This kind of attitude is more or less fully supported by authors like Madina Tlostanova, who argues that postcolonialism has been applied to the study of former colonies during the Cold War period. Tlostanova insists that postcolonialism and postcommunism have a lot in common: "Both postcolonial and postcommunist discourses are products of modernity/coloniality, emphasizing different elements, yet having a common source ... and a shared birthmark in the rhetoric of modernity (the mission of progress, development, civilization, and so on) acting as a tool to justify the continuing colonization of time and space, of lives and futures."[11] She draws attention to the fact that both the Imperial Russian and Soviet empires attempted to introduce and pursue their own versions of globality or modernity; however, as Russian/Soviet modernity had to be adjusted to the European form, the result was often mimicry.[12]

In his introduction to a special issue of the *Central Asian Survey* focusing on post-Soviet/postcolonial Central Asia, Adeeb Khalid discussed several important aspects closely related to the status of the USSR and its imperial/colonial policies throughout the last century. He rightly observed that there are difficulties with a "straightforward comparison" between the Soviet Union and other colonial powers that we could call 'classical' (he does not use this particular term, though) as the Soviet regime essentially presented itself as an anti-colonial state supporting the decolonization of the Third World countries. At the same time, it regularly declared modernization and the "fight" against backwardness to be among its most essential goals. It could be added that Soviet ideology claimed that the ultimate role of Soviet communism was global as it aimed at a "proletarian revolution" that would take over the whole world. The Communist Party of the Soviet Union always insisted that it acted in the name of progress and the ultimate liberation of oppressed nations. Concluding his insights, Khalid aptly observed that

> We can no longer rejoice in any kind of certainty over what a 'real' colonial empire ought to look like. This has important consequences for our subject. The Soviet Union cannot simply be measured up against static definitions of empire or colonialism, nor will the mechanical 'application' of postcolonial theory developed elsewhere lead to fruitful insights. Rather, the Soviet case has a great deal to offer to the common endeavour of understanding the complexities of the history of the 20th century and of its aftermaths. Soviet history can broaden the horizons of postcolonial studies by introducing a vast array of historical and cultural encounters little known to the field, but the Soviet case can also inject new caveats and perhaps a new scepticism toward generalizations built on the basis of the experience of mainly bourgeois, western European overseas empires.[13]

What a number of scholars dealing with post-Soviet space have come to realize is that Imperial Russia and its successor, the Soviet Union, were big and ambiguous players in Eurasia that tried to maintain a strong grip on the countries closest to its borders, no matter their history or whether they were Muslim or Christian societies.

One could agree with Khalid about the ambiguity of certain terms. However, as he justly emphasized while studying the practice of Russo-Soviet imperial policies, it is possible to come up with accumulated knowledge that could contribute to reconsidering the theory and practice of colonization as well as rethinking the generally accepted models of colonialism and postcolonialism. Despite the growing consensus in acknowledging that Tsarist as well as Soviet Russia (which eventually became the Soviet Union) was both an imperialist and a colonial enterprise, their characters were different in certain respects (sometimes even more brutal) than most other known colonial regimes. This kind of clarification could contribute to the growing understanding that both imperialism and colonialism have many forms and faces.

Shifting Views on Baltic Postcolonialism

Despite some important and timely aid (like the project of globalizing postcolonial studies initiated by David Chioni Moore), the road taken by Baltic researchers toward postcolonialism was bumpy and not short of obstacles, especially in the first two decades after the collapse of the Soviet system. The reasons for these difficulties were both internal and external. There was little support (if any) in local academic circles, and accordingly, the authors applying a postcolonial framework to analyze their cultures, societies, and literatures were often unjustly criticized, institutionally silenced, or even ridiculed in academic circles and the public sphere. They continued to be dismissed as superficial, exotic, obsessed with obnoxious ideas imported from outside, and the like. Literary scholars who attempted to adopt postcolonialism as a research strategy for Baltic societies, especially in the first post-Soviet decade, were mostly ignored by their older and institutionally far more powerful peers. On the other hand, a few Baltic scholars in the US and Canada who adopted a postcolonial approach to studying different Baltic cultures and their literatures pursued individual projects that, during the early post-Soviet period, had little or no impact on the development of local research strategies.[14]

On the international level, however, Moore's call for the expansion of postcolonial studies to embrace the post-Soviet sphere triggered a lot of interest and support. Though sometimes considered quite provocative, his approach won support after his article "Is the Post- in Postcolonial the Post- in Post-Soviet? Toward a Global Postcolonial Critique" was published in the influential *Proceedings of the Modern Language Association* (later republished in *Baltic Postcolonialism*), encouraging literary scholars in the US, Canada, and eventually the Baltic states to use postcolonialism as an analytical tool to study post-communist cultures and societies.

In the case of post-Soviet Lithuania, some attempts to incorporate postcolonial criticism into local discourses were made as early as 1996. However, the call had little impact on literary scholars, who instead chose to pursue mainstream research agendas.[15] At that time, semiotics was considered to be the most promising tool of literary analysis mainly because of the influence of Algirdas Julien Greimas and a small yet influential group of local researchers who claimed they were following his scholarly agenda. Only a handful of scholars were interested in postcolonial theory or postcolonial studies, and this interest was generally discouraged by academic institutions and the state funding agencies run by their representatives. Moreover, institutionally, there was almost no space to pursue any research connected to the postcolonial agenda. In an article published in 1999, American Lithuanian literary scholar Violeta Kelertas made the following apt observation:

> Although much has been written about various locations and forms of postcolonialism, the empire that constituted the Soviet Union has been little discussed in these terms, and Baltic scholars, both in and outside the countries themselves, are only now beginning to realize the utility of this approach.[16]

Though there were definitely some scholars on both sides of the Atlantic who realized the potential of this approach, under these circumstances, there was no easy way for postcolonialism to enter the realm of Baltic and/or Lithuanian studies. This was especially true of the first post-Soviet decade, for which there were a number of reasons. Some of these reasons were local, while others were related to a more global context, briefly mentioned above. However, some further comments are needed to understand why postcolonial studies remained absent for such a long time.

During this period, the local literary scene in Lithuania (and elsewhere in Eastern Europe) was still institutionally dominated by the 'old timers' who were hardly eager to meet any new theoretical frameworks or adjust to any new interpretation agendas. Some established local scholars firmly believed that any new interpretative framework questioned or denied their earlier contributions to literary analysis or even threatened their institutional existence and, ultimately, survival. Such an attitude was shared by both the hardliners of Soviet literary scholarship as well as somewhat more liberal scholars who wholeheartedly embraced certain Western theories (e.g., semiotics) but remained hostile to those intellectual agendas that lacked long-term scholarly traditions. Local semioticians who had previously made timely contributions to the development of Lithuanian literary criticism, however, maintained a distance from scholars engaged in postcolonial studies.

The institutional context of literary studies also needs to be discussed. First of all, the structure and hierarchy of academic institutions in the early post-Soviet period mostly remained the same as in the late Soviet era, except that some funding was reduced. Thus, senior academics not only controlled university departments and other scholarly institutions (e.g., the Institute of Lithuanian Literature and Folklore, which previously belonged to the system of research institutes under the auspices of the Lithuanian Academy of Sciences before it became a separate research body) but also dominated other spheres. For instance, they sat on various committees that approved long-term research projects and had their say in the largest publishing houses by acting as advisors and experts. They were also significantly represented in different institutions that provided funds for publishing books, such as committees that functioned under the purview of the Ministry of Culture and controlled the dissemination of state funding to publishing scholarly books in the field of humanities. It was only much later that this role was taken over by the Lithuanian Culture Council, which became the main distributor of the state's financial resources to the publishing sphere. In this respect, it should be noted that even now, hardly any scholarly book in Lithuania appears without significant financial backing from the state, as even private publishers depend on state grants.

On the other hand, there were also practical issues. Younger scholars lacked proficiency in English and other foreign languages, and their possibilities to obtain higher education at Western universities were still rather limited. Besides, local academic journals and publishing houses were hardly eager to offer space for 'suspicious' and thus 'illegitimate' criticism and theorizing. To make matters worse, public funds supporting any new approaches in the humanities were scarce until the establishment of the Open Society Foundation, which offered an almost unique alternative to state funding.

The general lack of interest in new literary trends and theories can be well illustrated by my own personal experience. Sometime around 1996, I received a message from Professor Violeta Kelertas at the University of Illinois at Chicago about the visit of a young but already established American scholar, David Chioni Moore. While making a study field trip to Central Asia, he was supposed to stay in Vilnius and give a lecture on postcolonial studies and their uses at the Open Society Foundation. At Professor Kelertas' urging, I showed up for the lecture. However, to my surprise and dismay, I found out that I was one of only three persons who turned up for this highly publicized public event. However, this disappointment turned into a blessing as instead of a formal lecture, we left the Foundation's premises and went to a nearby coffee house. There, we spent a few hours engaged in a highly interesting, thought-provoking, and far less formal intellectual discussion. As a matter of fact, this exchange also triggered my own interest in postcolonial theory and especially its applicability to the study of Lithuanian literature during the post-communist era.

In the West, there were different reasons for a cold or even hostile attitude toward applying postcolonialism to the study of Eastern European literatures and cultures. This attitude can be scrutinized and explained with the benefit of the present-day perspective. For a long time after 1917, Soviet Russia fashioned and presented itself as an anti-imperialist state, a pioneering political entity, the epitome of social and political progress speaking for all the 'humiliated and overwhelmed' of the world and occasionally demonstrating its formal aid to African and Asian countries fighting against capitalism and colonialism. The West was trapped by its naïve and one-sided visions of Eastern Europe and the Soviet Union. These visions, of course, were influenced, in one way or another, by the reigning political climate and the domination of the intellectual Left, which had an ambiguous attitude toward communism and the Soviet Union. For example, while the renowned French intellectual Jean-Paul Sartre visited the Soviet Union and spent some time in the Baltic (Lithuania in particular) during this trip, meeting with local writers, the fact that he failed to acknowledge the ambiguities of Soviet reality is quite telling.

However, Sartre, who coincidentally wrote an excellent introduction to Albert Memi's book *The Colonizer and the Colonized*, was not alone in lacking an understanding or perhaps a willingness to acknowledge the true reality of the colonized Baltic countries. Hordes of Western intellectuals continued to be hypnotized by the achievements of 'really existing socialism' while simultaneously closing their eyes to deportations, Gulags, etc., writing these off as distortions of Stalinism. Many Western intellectuals were so entertained by the idea of communism that they cared little about what was really going on behind the Iron Curtain. Curiously enough, this openly apologetic view of Soviet Communism continued after World War II despite the availability of information about the crimes committed by the Soviet regime against people of subjugated countries and 'internal enemies.'

In his chapter in *Baltic Postcolonialism*, the American literary scholar Karlis Račevskis quotes a passage from *Les Temps modernes*, an influential French journal closely related to Sartre and his circle. These lines are full of both admiration of the communist regime and total ignorance of its true nature:

> There is no country in the world where the dignity of work is more respected than in the Soviet Union. Forced labor does not exist there, because the exploitation of man by man has long since been abolished. Workers enjoy the fruits of their own labor and are no longer forced to depend on a few capitalist exploiters. Forced labor is characteristic of the capitalist system because, in capitalist countries, workers are treated like slaves by their capitalist masters.[17]

Note that these equally misleading and delirious observations were published during the period when the Soviet Gulag system (no less based on the idea of forced labor than Nazi concentration camps) was reaching the peak of its expansion. What is perhaps even worse is that such distorted visions of the Soviet Union proliferated among intellectuals in most

Western societies, and, to a certain degree, they continued to exist even after Nikita Khrushchev exposed the atrocious crimes of the Stalinist era. One should also not forget that after a brief period of thaw, repressions against dissidents and internal critics of the regime resumed and continued until the collapse of the Soviet system.

One of the reasons for this curious blindness of Western intellectuals (together with the limited availability of accurate information) was the very character of the Soviet Union, which claimed it was supporting decolonization processes all over the globe and extended aid to a number of African and Asian states, albeit while having its own political interests that went beyond its rhetoric of anti-colonialism and anti-imperialism. Such doublespeak was applied not only in the internal affairs of the Soviet Union but also in its international rhetoric that managed to capture the imagination of naïve Western intellectuals, who took the hypocritical anti-imperialist rhetoric of Vladimir Lenin and his ideological heirs at face value. It took decades for Western intellectuals to realize that the allegedly anti-imperialist policies of the Soviet Union and its support for decolonizing Third World societies masked the deeply entrenched imperialist and colonialist nature of Soviet Russia and its successor, the Soviet Union, and its enormous appetite for swallowing its neighbors in Central Asia and the Baltic region.

When discussing the problems of extending postcolonialism to Eastern Europe, especially the Baltic states, some scholars have argued that there are several reasons for the general reluctance to see the countries of this region as victims of Russian and Soviet colonial policies. One of the reasons that often obscures this perspective is closely related to the genealogy of Western critical theory itself. Critical theory, which gave rise to postcolonial studies, was developed as a discourse of the Left, and thus it was not free from certain prejudices, especially in terms of viewing imperialism and colonialism as primarily a Western enterprise. For example, Račevskis, following Moore's insights, further elaborated on this issue, arguing that such an ambiguous attitude was an inevitable consequence of the Leftist discourse that dominated in the West:

> What complicates matters even further in the case of the Baltic states is that leftist critical theory in general is implicated in a long history of misperception or miscomprehension of the Soviet system. In this sense, it could indeed be said that the Baltic countries have been doubly disadvantaged: victims of World War II, they were further victimized by the Cold War that followed, since the latter prevented them from being seen as the victims of the former.[18]

Other contributors to *Baltic Postcolonialism* implicitly or explicitly shared this viewpoint and gave their insights into the imperialist and colonialist policies of Tsarist Russia and the Soviet Union and their relations with their closest neighbors. This timely collection of scholarly articles extended the arguments and insights previously made by Moore and, perhaps even more importantly, not only brought fresh interpretative schemes to the field of postcolonial studies but also made interesting and convincing linguistic, literary, and cultural material available to the students of this vast and constantly expanding research field. The book has attracted a lot of attention among postcolonial scholars, accumulated many generally favorable reviews, and continues to be widely quoted in Lithuania, where the book was surprisingly welcomed. The more than a dozen reviews that accompanied its publication contained mostly praise rather than rejection, skepticism, or suspicion. It looked like Baltic postcolonialism was finally accepted and approved both on the international scholarly scene as well as in the Baltic countries. It should be added in this context that in contrast to Lithuania, the application of postcolonial studies toward Baltic societies and cultures was somewhat more favorable in Estonia and Latvia even before this volume became available. Some reviewers saw the success of this book as the final and indisputable legitimation of the postcolonial approach to Baltic societies, cultures, and literatures. This bold conclusion, however, turned out to be at least a little premature.

Critical Theory Strikes Back

In an article published in the *Journal of Postcolonial Writing*, Neil Lazarus, a well-known postcolonial scholar from the UK, attacked Eastern European (and Baltic) scholarship for claiming its own space within the framework of postcolonial studies. He questioned the attempts to interpret post-Soviet literatures and cultures as belonging to postcolonial discourse and shared his doubts about whether the claims of Baltic scholars regarding their cultures as subjects of postcolonial inquiry were grounded and legitimate. However, Lazarus did not dispute the claim of Baltic (or any other) countries that they were victims of Russian colonialism and imperialism before 1917, i.e., the October Revolution that marked a new era and course in Russia's history.[19] Supporting this view, Lazarus even quoted a Russian historian, Vasily Klyuchevsky, who insisted back in 1911 (i.e., before the October Revolution) that colonization was "the most essential element" in Russia's history. Although he cited Klyuchevsky from Marc Ferro's book *Colonization: A Global History* rather than examining the original writings of the renowned Russian historian of the imperial period, Lazarus seems to fully agree that Imperial Russia was an empire that pursued colonial and imperialist policies and expanded its borders by force. In this sense, he implicitly sides with Edward Said, who made the above-mentioned observation about Tsarist Russia's role in colonizing the countries that were closest to its borders.

However, his approach toward the case of the Soviet Union was far more complex and complicated. While discussing the problematic aspects of the issue, Lazarus refers to Moore's article in which he observed the differences between Imperial Russia's and the Soviet Union's colonizing policies and practices. Nevertheless, Lazarus' further arguments represent a departure from Moore's position and his famous call for a 'global postcolonial critique.' For Lazarus, this project was too far-fetched and far too broad. Even Said's work was reassessed to insist that postcolonialism was and continues to be related to the West rather than "specific dynamics of capitalist development."[20]

> Because of their third-worldist presuppositions, postcolonial scholars seldom give sufficient emphasis to the fact that, whatever else it might have and, indeed, did involve – all the way from the cultivation of aesthetic tastes and preferences to the systematic annihilation of whole communities – colonialism as an historical process involved the forced integration of hitherto uncapitalized societies, or societies in which the capitalist mode of production was not hegemonic, in to a capitalist world-system. Over the course of a couple of centuries in some territories, mere decades in others, generalized commodity production was imposed, monetization; the development of specifically capitalist markets (involving "free" wage labour and the bullying and selling of labour power), or the appropriation, de- and re-centralizing of existing markets, and of ancillary systems and institutions designed to enable and facilitate the consolidation, extension and reproduction of capitalist production and capitalist class relations. Along the way, existing social relations and modes of existence were undermined, destroyed, reconfigured; new social relations and modes of existence were brought into being.[21]

Lazarus seems to be concerned with both 'third-worldism' and especially the reductionist character of some mainstream postcolonial narratives and the post-communist critique that embraces postcolonialism for its own purposes. Yet he repeatedly questions the validity and legitimacy of post-Soviet studies to appropriate methods and interpretative schemes used by postcolonial scholars. In one of the notes accompanying his article, he shares his fear that the demise of Soviet dominance and the communist system might discredit the very idea of communism as wrong, as "historical lessons" might be drawn from the experiences of its former dominance and its end.[22]

Suggesting that there is "a world of difference" between post-Marxist postcolonial theory and the "post-communism" of those scholars reflecting upon the changes in the post-Soviet realm, Lazarus goes on to explain his explicit distrust of applying postcolonial theory to the study of countries subjugated by the Soviet Union:

> It is perfectly possible, however, both to celebrate the "independence" gained or regained with the collapse of the Soviet system and to recognize that the "freedom" won in 1989 and the years immediately following has not been unqualified. The various decolonizations achieved in the Bandung era enabled formerly colonial societies to represent themselves as nation states in a world of nation states. But what was not adequately registered until later was that this world of nation states was a radically unequal one, structured in dominance, so that what continues to be celebrated in the various Independence Days is rarely "independence" as that term is commonly understood. Similarly, in the post-Soviet contexts, the full implication of the fact that liberation from "actually existing" socialism had been liberation into the world-system of "really existing" capitalism are now having to be confronted. For this latter is a world-system, already and in principle deeply uneven, and now undergoing profound contraction and structural crisis besides.[23]

Such an attitude reflects the caution quite typical of some Western scholars in assessing the applicability of postcolonial discourse to societies dominated by the Soviet Union. As mentioned earlier, this reluctant attitude toward expanding the notion of postcolonialism so as to accommodate Eastern European cultures and societies labeled 'post-Soviet' after 1990 can be explained by the Leftist origin and development of postcolonial theory, as Kelertas and other contributors to *Baltic Postcolonialism* discussed.

However, it should be added that some Eastern European scholars share a reserved – if not an overtly skeptical – attitude toward the 'globalization' of postcolonialism. Such scholars have their own reasons for rejecting its geographical expansion and especially its use as an intellectual tool to study Central and Eastern European societies. For example, Romanian literary scholar Andrei Terian insists that "in order to become a truly efficient analytical instrument, postcolonialism requires integration in a unified theory of (inter)literary dependence and, at the same time, it must be dissociated from certain concepts that concern interrelated phenomena, such as imperialism, domination or oppression."[24] Speaking in similar tones to Lazarus, Terian rejects the very possibility of applying postcolonial theory to explain processes that Eastern European cultures and societies underwent during the period of the Cold War and Soviet domination in the region as well as in conditions that came into being when this region escaped the 'guardianship' of Soviet internationalism. Taking a reserved attitude toward the conceptualization of postcolonialism as a global intellectual toolbox, Terian fears that there is "the risk to simply equate postcolonialism with any form of dependency/domination. However, such a possibility, far from emphasizing the crucial importance of postcolonial studies in the current humanities (in the form of the so-called 'global postcolonial critique' envisioned by David Chioni Moore), would in fact cancel the utility of the concept."[25] Curiously, despite refusing to embrace postcolonial studies as an intellectual tool suitable for the analysis of Europe's East, Terian, unlike Lazarus, acknowledges the legitimacy of Baltic postcolonialism.

Other scholars, such as the Russian literary historian and critic Evgeny Dobrenko, continue to deny the legitimacy of applying postcolonial theory to the study of the post-Soviet realm (and the Baltic countries in particular). When Dobrenko took part in a conference organized in Vilnius and eventually in a discussion on methods in literary scholarship, he claimed:

> [Postcolonialism] does not always work, this theory is too big – it tries to cover everything from Mumbai to Kinshasa, from Moscow to Vilnius, so here is a problem. The same can be said not only about postcolonialism, but about all grandeur, megalomania theories. Structuralism is a different thing, it is instrumental. Theories like postcolonialism, gender studies, postmodernism are ideologically situated grand theories. And because structuralism is instrumental, it is much more practical in our real work and can be accepted by a much wider audience. These grand theories very often don't have the methodological apparatus and instruments that can be used specifically for our purposes when it comes to specific material. They are too much politically biased.[26]

Such an opinion is hardly new to any student of Baltic postcolonialism. As I have already discussed, attempts to redirect postcolonial studies toward the post-Soviet space and analyze the historical consequences of Russian and Soviet colonialism and imperialism have been met with attitudes of reservation, open skepticism, and, occasionally, distrust and utmost dissatisfaction. Some reservations are understandable, and some are, perhaps, even well-grounded. What is striking, however, is that the opponents of Baltic postcolonialism choose to bypass some important arguments provided by scholars developing postcolonial studies in the Baltics. For some reason, certain articulations remain neither taken into consideration nor seriously reconsidered, such as the statements of Karl J. Jirgens when he insisted that

The Balts can be analyzed in postcolonial terms not only as victims of the Soviet occupation, but as victims of earlier imperialist occupations spanning over one thousand years at the hands of the Teutonic Knights, the Germanic invaders, Tsarist Russian forces, and so on. It should be carefully noted that Lithuania's situation over the past millennium is somewhat different from that of Estonia and Latvia in that Lithuania as the Grand Duchy also partook in colonization, but at other times, like Latvia and Estonia, fell victim to more powerful forces. To exclude the Balts from any postcolonial discussion not only overlooks then centuries of recurring colonial activity, but extends the effects of oppression against these nations by deflecting or muzzling open debate.[27]

Nevertheless, attempts to eliminate any kind of research on Baltic postcolonialism raise various sorts of questions. By no means the least of these is why redirecting postcolonial studies toward the post-Soviet space causes so much inconvenience to some Eastern European scholars who, unlike some of their colleagues in the Western hemisphere, have been exposed to experiences of Soviet imperialism and colonialism.

Instead of providing an answer to this complex question at this point, I will conclude this consideration with a glimpse at the current state of the art in what, in geographical terms, might be viewed as an emerging and developing sub-field of postcolonial studies. However, before proceeding with this topic, it is worth briefly considering some postcolonial criticism that does not support a view suggesting that postcolonial necessarily "requires integration in a unified theory of (inter)literary dependence," as Terian has claimed. For example, Albert J. Paolini notes that this approach is essentially different from other standard critical theories. According to Paolini,

> Indeed, to refer to postcolonialism as a discourse is misleading in itself. Because it encompasses differing perspectives and theoretical inputs, postcolonialism is not a uniform body of writing. It includes distinct movements and overlapping concerns, a fact that makes a delineation between the central tropes of difference, resistance, ambivalence and hybridity extremely difficult. Some writers tend to emphasize both difference and hybridity, resistance and ambivalence. Others, like Said, have subtly changed their perspective over time, so that hybridity has received more permanent guernsey.[28]

Other authors note that postcolonial studies have never aspired to the role of some meta-theory that has developed rigid intellectual instruments to analyze its objects of study and set out clear and indisputable boundaries. A sound and promising approach was offered by Bill Ashcroft, who insists that postcolonialism "was never a grand theory, but as a methodology; first, for analysing the many strategies by which colonized societies have engaged imperial discourse; and second, for studying the ways in which many of those strategies are shared by colonized societies, re-emerging in very different political and cultural circumstances."[29]

There are, of course, other ways of looking at postcolonialism and understanding as well as making use of its ambivalences and the certain fluidity of its boundaries, which remain more open than closed. As an intellectual instrument, postcolonialism provides a lot of possibilities for practitioners who are ready to move the boundaries of discourse. As Bart Moore-Gilbert has argued, postcolonialism

> helped to undermine the traditional conception of disciplinary boundaries. Configurations such as 'colonial discourse analysis' insist upon the importance of studying literature together with history, politics, sociology and other forms rather than isolation from the multiple material and intellectual contexts which determine its production and reception. In related fashion, postcolonial criticism has challenged hitherto dominant notions of the autonomy of the aesthetic sphere, helping to gain acceptance for the argument, advanced on a number of fronts since the 1960s especially, that 'culture' mediates relations of power as effectively, albeit in more indirect and subtle ways, as more public and visible forms of oppression.[30]

Baltic Postcolonialism: Beyond Exaltation and Denial

There are different ways of viewing and reconsidering the ongoing project of Baltic postcolonialism, which still has both supporters and critics. One possible attitude is to continue to question not only its accomplishments but also its legitimacy and premises, as some of the authors previously mentioned have repeatedly done, albeit without providing any convincing and unquestionable arguments.

On the other hand, unlike in the case of the so-called 'hard sciences,' humanities are full of different and sometimes inconsistent or even incompatible arguments. Such rivalry while debating which particular discourse is most appropriate to the analysis of Baltic culture and society during and after the (colonial) dependence is nothing new. In fact, it has gone on since the Baltic countries re-established their independence and made attempts to find their way toward what we might call the regime of Western liberal democracy.

After a lengthy period of ignoring postcolonial studies/postcolonial theory as one of the many possible intellectual tools for analyzing these societies, postcolonialism finally found its way to Eastern Europe and the

Baltics in particular. After being denied, ignored, and later marginalized, in the last two decades, postcolonialism has finally entered local academic discourses in the Baltic societies despite the many challenges it has faced and most probably will continue to meet in the future. Having originated within the circles of literary scholars (and despite still being mostly ignored within the discipline of history), it is winning more and more ground in various disciplinary and sub-disciplinary fields, like folkloristics. As Latvian scholar Toms Kencis recently argued:

> A postcolonial approach to Soviet-era Baltic folkloristics looks beneficial in many ways. It provides a toolkit for deep analysis of the disciplinary field, a solid theoretical foundation via adaptation and update of colonial folkloristics, and a vocabulary that allows capturing ambivalent, multivocal echoes of the past in today's scholarship. It is a model that simultaneously hosts different meanings of the research object and thus represents it closer to the actual historical complexity. It also promises to liberate the scholarship from outdated distinctions and oppositions native to the Cold War and its tripartite world division.[31]

Despite what the staunchest critics of Baltic postcolonialism say, there is no doubt that the application of this theoretical agenda has already proved meaningful and quite effective in analyzing Baltic cultures and literatures during the Imperial Russian and Soviet colonization processes and beyond. Perhaps the main issue today is not the legitimacy of this analytical and interpretative discourse but the uneven development of postcolonial critique in the Baltic realm. Scholars of Latvia and especially Estonia seem to have embraced postcolonial studies with the least prejudice, and consequently, they have produced somewhat more research for international readers.[32] Though traces of postcolonial theory might be found in various dissertations, books, and book chapters focused on Lithuanian culture, postcolonialism is still marginalized to a certain degree as a theoretical framework in Lithuanian literary and cultural scholarship and remains almost entirely ignored in the communities of historians. Perhaps more efforts are needed to change its current position on the map of Lithuanian scholarship, especially because this intellectual agenda is capable of opening prospects not only for literary studies but also for a number of other scholarly disciplines.

However, it is most likely that despite its potential, postcolonialism will remain on the margins of cultural and especially historical research inside Lithuania for several reasons, the discussion of which is beyond the scope of the present chapter. As I have previously emphasized, attitudes toward postcolonial studies among scholars researching various aspects of history, culture, and society have generally been more favorable in Latvia and Estonia; however, overcoming this marginalization in Lithuania remains a vital intellectual project worth conscious effort. It should also be remembered that all three Baltic states fell prey to their more powerful neighbors' pursuits of their colonialist and imperialist policies in various historical periods, including the twentieth century. Dealing with their colonial past and analyzing various aspects of their societies thus remains an important goal for both the present and the future.

The ongoing project of the postcolonial analysis of Baltic culture and societies needs to be pursued, especially when discussing the changes in regional and international socio-cultural and political contexts, as Benedikts Kalnačs has emphasized:

> The place of Baltic societies and cultures and their future in this positive framework of potentially rising new regionalism is, however, far from being established and safe. The inhabitants of the respective countries are again confronted with their already familiar experience of being situated in the sphere of tension in between major powers, as Baltic societies still find themselves in a place – both physically and mentally – between "civilizations." Herein also lies the paradox of their "colonial present," as this specific situation seems to be ignored even by postcolonial studies which has, generally speaking, dislocated Estonia, Latvia and Lithuania to the sidelines of history – this time as "internal others" of the Western civilization.[33]

Despite the continuous silence of postcolonial scholarship toward the Baltics and their historical and cultural experience, attempts to study the historical legacy of this geographical area as well as its present are meaningful. The previous silence has already been broken by a number of voices insisting on applying the postcolonial perspective to Baltic studies, and there is now a growing number of scholars both inside Lithuania, Latvia, and Estonia as well as outside who have realized not only the utility and potential of this approach (on which Kelertas insisted in her ground-breaking volume) but also the legitimacy of addressing these issues within the framework of postcolonialism.[34] Nevertheless, there is a lot to be done in the near as well as more distant future. First, Baltic scholars need to convince their colleagues working on other regions and continents about the importance of analyzing and interpreting the cultures, histories, and societies of this region in terms of postcolonial theory. They also need to persuade their colleagues in other disciplines (like history and sociology) about the importance of applying a postcolonial outlook to the legacy and present context of the Baltics.

It seems that the moment to fully embrace the postcolonial approach in the Baltics is more than timely and adequate, especially as Russia's recent aggression and war against Ukraine exposed its true nature as an imperialist state that has not managed to face or deal with its colonial past. Russia's ongoing imperialist war against Ukraine and its regular threats against the Baltic countries testify that the small group of scholars who set their eyes on postcolonialism as an important part of an intellectual toolbox to analyze their societies and cultures almost two decades ago were not only ahead of their time but were timely, accurate, and insightful in their approach. Further developing the postcolonial analysis of Baltic cultures, societies, and literatures is full of potential to highlight this region's most pressing internal and external problems.

It should be added that adopting a postcolonial perspective on the post-Soviet space is now getting more supporters than a couple of decades ago. A recent publication discussing post-Soviet legislation in purely postcolonial terms contributes to a growing list of literature related to Baltic and Eastern European postcolonialism.[35] Scholars researching Eastern Europe, especially sociologists, have provided well-argued opinions on the benefits of postcolonial analysis and successfully applied key categories of postcolonialism to their objects of study.[36] There is no reason why Lithuanian society, culture, and literature cannot be subjected to such studies that, so far, have been pursued by individual and loosely connected researchers.

Notes

[1] Said, *Culture and Imperialism*, xxii.

[2] Ibid, xxiii.

[3] Chamberlain, *Decolonization,* 97.

[4] Moore, "Is the Post- in Postcolonial the Post- in Post-Soviet?," 17.

[5] Ibid, 17–18.

[6] Verdery, "Nationalism, Postsocialism, and Space in Eastern Europe," 77–95.

[7] Verdery, "Whither Postsocialism?," 15–22.

[8] Korek, "Central and Eastern Europe from a Postcolonial Perspective."

[9] Carey and Raciborski, "Postcolonialism," 206.

[10] Adams, "Can We Apply Postcolonial Theory to Central Eurasia," 3.

[11] Tlostanova, "Postsocialist ≠ Postcolonial," 132.

[12] Ibid, 135.

[13] Khalid, "Introduction," 471.

[14] A paper discussing the state of the art in Lithuanian literary studies delivered by Violeta Kelertas in 1996 during an annual convention of the short-lived World Community of Lithuanian Scholars (Pasaulio lituanistų bendrija) established in Vilnius in 1994 by Prof. Albertas Zalatorius triggered some discussions but

generally had no lasting impact upon local development in Lithuanian literary studies. See Kelertas, "Lengvai pučia keturi vėjai lietuvių literatūrologijoje," 65–76.
[15] Samalavičius, "Postkomunizmo studijų klausimu," 11–14.
[16] Kelertas, "Perceptions of the Self and the Other," 251.
[17] Račevskis, "Toward the Postcolonial Perspective on the Baltic States," 171
[18] Ibid.
[19] Lazarus, "Spectres Haunting," 117–129.
[20] Ibid, 120.
[21] Ibid, 120.
[22] Ibid, 127.
[23] Ibid, 121.
[24] Terian, "Is There an East-Central European Postcolonialism?," 21.
[25] Ibid, 26.
[26] See Evgeny Dobrenko's contribution at the conference "The Literary Field under Communist Regime: Structure, Functions, Illusions," held in Vilnius from October 7–9, 2015; published as Dobrenko, "A Discussion on Methodology for Researching Soviet Literary Space," 149–162.
[27] Jirgens, "Fusions of Discourse," 47.
[28] Paolini, *Navigating Modernity*, 52.
[29] Ashcroft, *Post-Colonial Transformations*, 7.
[30] Moore-Gilbert, *Postcolonial Theory*, 8.
[31] Kencis, "Baltic Postcolonialism," 23.
[32] See Annus, *Soviet Postcolonial Studies*; Annus, ed., *Coloniality, Nationality, Modernity*; Kalnačs, "Latvian Multiculturalism, Postcolonialism and World Literature"; Hanovs, "Can Postcolonial Theory Help Explain Latvian Politics of Integration?"
[33] Kalnačs, "Latvian Multiculturalism, Postcolonialism and World Literature."
[34] See Kelertas, *Kita vertus*; Cidzikaitė, *Kitas lietuvių prozoje*; Samalavičius, "Kas bijo postkolonializmo studijų?," 153–162; Samalavičius, "Postkolonializmas ir postkomunistinės Lietuvos kultūra"; Samalavičius, "Beyond Nostalgia," 14–25.
[35] See Parteltt and Kupper, *The Post-Soviet as Post-Colonial*.
[36] See, e.g., Owczarzak, "Introduction"; Mayblin et al., "Other' Posts in 'Other' Places."

Works Cited

Adams, Laura L. "Can We Apply Postcolonial Theory to Central Eurasia?" *Central Eurasian Studies Review* 7, no. 1 (2008): 1–7.
—. *Soviet Postcolonial Studies*. New York: Routledge, 2017.
Annus, Epp, ed. *Coloniality, Nationality, Modernity: A Postcolonial View on Baltic Culture under Soviet Rule*. New York: Routledge, 2018.
Ashcroft, Bill. *Post-Colonial Transformations*. London: Routledge, 2001.
Carey, Henry F., and Rafal Raciborski. "Postcolonialism: A Valid Paradigm for the Former Sovietized States and Yugoslavia?" *East European Politics and Societies* 18, no. 2 (2004): 191–235.

Chamberlain, Muriel E. *Decolonization: The Fall of the European Empires.* Oxford: Blackwell, 1999.

Cidzikaitė, Dalia. *Kitas lietuvių prozoje.* Vilnius: Lietuvių literatūros ir tautosakos institutas, 2007.

Dobrenko, Evgeny. "A Discussion on Methodology for Researching Soviet Literary Space." *Colloquia* 35 (2015): 149–162.

Hanovs, Deniss. "Can Postcolonial Theory Help Explain Latvian Politics of Integration? Reflections on Contemporary Latvia as a Postcolonial Society." *Journal of Baltic Studies* 47, no. 1 (2016): 133–153.

Jirgens, Karl E. "Fusions of Discourse: Postcolonial/Postmodern Horizons in Baltic Culture." In *Baltic Postcolonialism*, edited by Violeta Kelertas, 45–81. Amsterdam/New York: Rodopi, 2006.

Kalnačs, Benedikts. "Latvian Multiculturalism, Postcolonialism and World Literature." In *World Literature and the Postcolonial: Narratives of (Neo) Colonialization in a Globalized World*, edited by Elke Sturm-Trigonakis, 159–170. Heidelberg: J. B. Metzler, 2020.

Kelertas, Violeta. "Lengvai pučia keturi vėjai lietuvių literatūrologijoje." In *Lituanistika XXI amžiaus išvakarėse: tyrinėjimų prioritetai, metodai ir naujovės*, edited by Albertas Zalatorius. Vilnius: Pasaulio lituanistų bendrija, 1997.

—. *Kita vertus: straipsniai apie lietuvių literatūrą.* Vilnius: baltos lankos, 2006.

—. "Perceptions of the Self and the Other in Lithuanian Postcolonial Fiction." In *Baltic Postcolonialism*, edited by Violeta Kelertas, 251–269. Amsterdam/New York: Rodopi, 2006.

Kencis, Toms. "Baltic Postcolonialism: A Prospect for Disciplinary History of Folkloristics." *Lettonica* 43 (2001): 8–29.

Khalid, Adeeb. "Introduction: Locating the (Post-)Colonial in Soviet History." *Central Asian Survey* 26, no. 4 (2007): 465–473.

Korek, Janusz. "Central and Eastern Europe from a Postcolonial Perspective." In *From Sovietology to Postcoloniality: Poland and Ukraine from a Postcolonial Perspective*, edited by Janusz Korek. Huddinge: Södertörns högskola, 2007.

Lazarus, Neil. "Spectres Haunting: Postcommunism and Postcolonialism." *Journal of Postcolonial Writing* 48, no. 2 (2012): 117–129.

Mayblin, Lucy, Aneta Piekut, and Gill Valentine. "'Other' Posts in 'Other' Places: Poland through a Postcolonial Lens?" *Sociology* 50, no. 1 (2016): 60–76.

Moore, David Chioni. "Is the Post- in Postcolonial the Post- in Post-Soviet?" In *Baltic Postcolonialism*, edited by Violeta Kelertas, 11–43. Amsterdam/New York: Rodopi, 2006.

Moore-Gilbert, Bart. *Postcolonial Theory: Contexts, Practices, Politics.* London: Verso, 1997.

Owczarzak, Jill. "Introduction: Postcolonial Studies and Postsocialism in Eastern Europe." *Focaal* 53, no. 3 (2009): 3–19.

Paolini, Albert. J. *Navigating Modernity: Postcolonialism, Identity and International Relations.* Boulder, CO: Lynne Rienner, 1999.

Partlett, William, and Herbert Kupper. *The Post-Soviet as Post-Colonial: A New Paradigm for Understanding Constitutional Dynamics in the Former Soviet Empire.* Northampton, MA: Edward Elgar, 2002.

Račevskis, Karlis. "Toward a Postcolonial Perspective on the Baltic States." In *Baltic Postcolonialism,* edited by Violeta Kelertas, 165–186. Amsterdam.New York: Rodopi, 2006.

Said, Edward. *Culture and Imperialism.* New York: Vintage Books, 1994.

Samalavičius, Almantas. "Beyond Nostalgia: Notes on History and Memory of the Soviet Era in Lithuanian Postcolonial Fiction." In *History, Memory and Nostalgia in Literature and Culture,* edited by Regina Rudaitytė, 14–24. Newcastle upon Tyne: Cambridge Scholars Publishing, 2018.

—. "Kas bijo postkolonializmo studijų?" In Almantas Samalavičius, *Kaita ir tęstinumas: kultūros kritikos esė,* 153–162. Vilnius: Kultūros barai, 2008.

—. "Postkolonializmas ir postkomunistinės Lietuvos kultūra." *Metmenys* 76 (1999): 151–167.

—. "Postkomunizmo studijų klausimu." *Kultūros barai* 11 (1996): 11–14.

Terian, Andrei. "Is There an East-Central European Postcolonialism? Toward a Unified Theory of (Inter)Literary Dependence." *World Literature Studies* 3, no. 21 (2012): 21–36.

Tlostanova, Madina. "Postsocialist ≠ Postcolonial? On Post-Soviet Imaginary and Global Coloniality." *Journal of Postcolonial Writing* 48, no. 2 (2012): 130–142.

Verdery, Catherine. "Nationalism, Postsocialism, and Space in Eastern Europe." *Social Research* 63, no. 1 (1996): 77–95.

—. "Whither Postsocialism?" In *Postsocialism: Ideals, Ideologies and Practices in Eurasia,* edited by C. M. Hann, 15–22. London: Routledge, 2002.

CHAPTER II

UNCANNY BEAUTY:
VILNIUS POKER BY RIČARDAS GAVELIS

Ričardas Gavelis (1950–2002) became a household name in Lithuania as soon as his acclaimed novel *Vilnius Poker* was published in 1989. The book quickly became a bestseller, selling an impressive amount of almost 100,000 copies across two editions published during the same year, catapulting its author to the center of both public attention and literary life. This was a transitory period when Lithuania was resolutely moving toward independence, eventually becoming the first country to say farewell to the Soviet Union and the communist regime. Gavelis' extended moment of fame came several years after his novel's publication: he gave dozens of interviews to the daily press, regularly appeared on TV, and wrote columns for the leading newspapers and magazines. His book was reviewed several dozen times, and although most dismissed the novel as highly offensive, anti-Lithuanian, exhibitionist, or even pornographic, they all contributed to the making of his name.

Hordes of bewildered, over-excited, and angry literary critics set out to smash his literary visions to pieces, blaming the author of *Vilnius Poker* for almost every imaginable sin. They saw no place for him in Lithuanian literature, which was coincidentally slowly and painfully recovering from the Soviet oppression and censorship that had lasted more than half a century. Meanwhile, readers were busily buying the book, emptying the shelves of the public libraries, and eagerly talking about the variety of subjects and themes discussed in *Vilnius Poker*. In fact, for several decades, many of its themes (including sex and perversion) were considered taboo and thus remained beyond the reach of any serious literature.

Immediately after *Vilnius Poker* was published, Gavelis, who had previously written several collections of generally well-received short stories and was considered a new voice in Lithuanian prose writing, became both a celebrity on a national scale and, at the same time, a highly controversial figure, admired by some and hated by others. Many of his fellow writers, envying his fame and popularity, sided with his critics and refused to accept his powerful literary visions.

The Writer and His Critics

As I have emphasized elsewhere,[1] Ričardas Gavelis was one of the leading Lithuanian prose writers of the late Soviet and early post-Soviet period who undoubtedly contributed significantly to the change of contemporary Lithuanian prose's themes, scope, narratives, and language, even when his popularity waned or when he came to be bypassed by some leading and influential academic critics. His novels and short stories were especially provocative and non-conformist in the Soviet era, and he was the first to openly introduce narratives about the Gulag experience and other forms of structural oppression. His most famous novel, *Vilnius Poker*, shook and changed the national literary landscape at the very end of the Soviet regime. It will quite possibly be viewed one day as one of the most exceptional pieces of literature written during the long period of censorship and control that lasted from World War II to the fall of the Soviet regime in 1990. Nevertheless, some further comments are needed here: he continued to be a bold and fierce critic of the post-Soviet reality, refusing to take any political or social discourse connected to these changes for granted. Additionally, he had a deep distrust of politicians as well as the ideologies that fuelled the chaotic and often contradictory politics of the post-communist era. This uncompromising attitude made him a lot of enemies both in the literary milieu and outside it.

As often happens with truly epochal writers, Gavelis was inadequately interpreted and understood during his lifetime. He was often comfortably labeled as a scandalous or popular author with a taste for sexual images, especially during those years when he challenged the murky literary landscape of Soviet Lithuania with his powerful images of the waning of historical Vilnius, the city he provocatively chose to label 'the ass of the universe.' Unlike other writers who reserved their criticism for the era that ended with the fall of the Soviet Union, Gavelis continued to write perceptive novels focused on ambiguous societal transformations and the new realignment of power after the reestablishment of Lithuania's independence. This kind of literary discourse happened to be against the liking of the country's literary establishment, the members of which had built their careers under the previous regime. Quite naturally, most of the Lithuanian literary critics of the time failed to grasp his literary images adequately and chose either to ignore or to attack his literary imagination as soon as *Vilnius Poker* was published, particularly since this novel aimed at destroying a number of cultural taboos and icons that had been beyond any critical scrutiny during the colonial era.

It is not at all surprising that even though it is almost thirty years since Gavelis' novels *Vilnius Poker* and *Memoirs of a Life Cut Short* were published and these exceptional literary works have finally been acknowledged as essential contributions to Lithuanian literature (especially after *Vilnius Poker* made its way onto the international literary market), his later novels, written and published after Lithuania gained its independence, continue to be considered far less important or even as failures. The opinion of literary scholar and critic Regimantas Tamošaitis is quite typical in this respect. He dismissed *Sun-Tzu's Life in the Holy City of Vilnius* as soon as it was published and dismissed Gavelis' several later novels as professionally composed and structured but otherwise absolutely exhausted. A few years ago, while discussing the development of contemporary Lithuanian prose in the country's leading literary journal *Metai* (coincidentally, Gavelis once served as its associate editor), Tamošaitis insisted:

> Ričardas Gavelis was angry and real. But then something happened to him as he started jazzing while searching for a new language, as if trying to find a way out of a literary dead-end with the help of various forms of suicide [the critic is here referring to one of Gavelis' later titles – A.S.]. His prose became too personal, too bitter, as if it were a way of dealing with his past. Gavelis' narration became lighter and faster, the metaphors more transparent and more impressive. When everything about our life in the Ass of the Universe had been said, his writing became a repetition of continuously grotesque metaphors, saying nothing new, but strengthening the effect of sensation and the sensual, increasing its grotesque character.[2]

Professor Vytautas Kubilius – a highly influential literary scholar and critic of the Soviet and early post-Soviet period – expressed his open dissatisfaction and even distaste for Gavelis' narration in an essay on the aesthetics of ugliness that, according to him, was taking root in post-Soviet Lithuanian prose writing. Curiously, despite being quite an insightful and perceptive critic who accumulated his symbolic capital as a supposedly non-conformist author of the Soviet era who was subjected to the attacks of the Soviet establishment (because of this, he was respected both by writers and by the general audience), Kubilius failed to see anything exceptional about *Vilnius Poker* except its supposedly low style and the brutal manner peculiar to the novel's narrative. The critic was appalled both by the imagery as well as by its brutal language. Kubilius insisted that,

> Ričardas Gavelis looks back at the same environment with a bridge of disgust and denial. "Faceless people," a "flow of the dead" run through the

streets. Someone is constantly watching and following you. Instead of the
altar, a bed of excrement was built, where "rich white worms are writhing"
– let's pray! A deranged patient swallows a "steaming, smelly sausage" of
his own excrement. In the cemetery, the head of the buried gravedigger splits
open, and "black steam kept coming out of the cracks in the coffin" <…>
"My city is dead and will never rise again," decides the protagonist of *Vilnius
Poker*. Above the Gediminas Tower and the Great Street hung a "fog of
meek, slimy fear," and "liquid shit flows through the veins of the great
people." Ričardas Gavelis develops the naturalistic description into
grotesque generalizations of the Soviet era and symbols of the omnipotence
of evil.[3]

Kubilius downplayed Gavelis' literary achievement and interpreted this
significant novel as a marginal piece of literature hardly worth the serious
consideration of a literary scholar. His emphasis on the "grotesque
generalizations of the Soviet era" demonstrates that Kubilius ignored or
completely misunderstood Gavelis' powerful message as well as the novel's
future impact upon Lithuanian prose writing. This kind of treatment of
Vilnius Poker and Gavelis' later novels seems to have met with the approval
of Lithuanian literary criticism, which has always tended to bypass or
underrate this truly exceptional Lithuanian writer, remaining hostile to his
innovative aesthetics and unsettling postcolonial narrative.

Though the reception of Gavelis' writings has changed considerably
during recent decades, a strange hostility prevails among a number of
literary critics who either refuse to acknowledge his impact on Lithuanian
literature or (more recently) choose to depreciate his later novels as
somewhat journalistic and repetitive. Such an attitude is exemplified in a
recent overview of Lithuanian prose writing by the translator, literary critic,
and recipient of the Vytautas Kubilius Prize, Laimantas Jonušys, who, while
discussing the tendencies of Lithuanian prose writing of the last twenty
years, chose to bypass the novels and short story collections by Ričardas
Gavelis altogether, dismissing his later writings as aesthetically non-
important arguing formally that they belong to an older period.[4] This sort of
attitude is perhaps not surprising, bearing in mind the tense and complex
history of relations between Lithuanian literary critics (both academic and
non-academic) and Gavelis' literary texts since the publication of *Vilnius
Poker*.

It should be added that it is only due to the efforts of Professor Violeta
Kelertas and a handful of literary scholars residing in Lithuania that
attitudes toward his writings finally shifted, especially after his novels were
extensively analyzed in a pioneering collection of literary and cultural
criticism analyzing Baltic texts from a postcolonial perspective. This timely
and significant volume of scholarship, titled *Baltic Postcolonialism* and

edited by Kelertas, had an undeniable influence on, among other things, the reception of Gavelis' prose writing in Lithuania. Consequently, his major novels could no longer be labeled as pornographic or belonging to mass culture, though these labels often continued to haunt his writings for more than a decade after *Vilnius Poker* was published.[5]

More recently, some scholars have chosen a different approach while trying to assess the impact of Gavelis' later writings. For example, literary critic Jūratė Čerškutė, whose Ph.D. thesis focused on Gavelis' prose writings, offered a different (though not at all novel) perspective on his literary career. According to Čerškutė:

> A black hole came into Lithuanian literature after Ričardas Gavelis died in August 2002 and Jurgis Kunčinas passed away at the beginning of December of the same year. These two unique writers cannot be replaced by anyone. Even now, twelve years after the death of Ričardas Gavelis, I can't find any other cultural and social critique.[6]

Though I would be inclined to disagree with her emphasis on the supposed lack of cultural and social critique after Gavelis passed away, especially as far as non-fictional literary forms are concerned, I share her musings about the black hole that was created in Lithuanian prose writing after his death. Unlike the majority of Lithuanian prose writers, who were and are most often dealing with their own personal and private experiences, Gavelis always aimed at offering society far more essential and significant metaphors. However, in a postscript to one of his later novels, he wrote that since it is not possible to draw any metaphor for life in post-Soviet society, the only remaining possibility is to write a criminal narrative. This overcooked statement seems to be his posture rather than creative credo.

On the other hand, Gavelis made good use of the criminal material that life after communism offered, especially in the first post-Soviet decade, when Lithuania was plagued by criminal gangs, racketeering, money laundering, and collapsing banks. However, he was wise enough to transcend this kind of journalistic narrative and was always concerned with more complex issues: why do human beings become the willing victims of their own enthusiasm while submitting themselves to new configurations of power that are no less evil than the previous one? Why do they fall prey to political and social manipulations by creating hordes of heroes and idols and following them uncritically, reducing free will and intellect to sloganeering and other forms of social mimicry?

Among many other things, Gavelis was concerned with the lack of intellectualism in Lithuanian prose – an issue he brilliantly and thoroughly discussed in *A Memoir of a Life Cut Short*, one of his first novels. His dissatisfaction with Lithuanian literature and Lithuanian intellectual culture in general naturally earned him many critics and enemies, who took his provocative musings personally and literally. Nevertheless, the issue of Lithuanian literature's anti-intellectualism remains as significant today as it was during Gavelis' lifetime.

Inside the Guts of *Vilnius Poker*

The reception of *Vilnius Poker* in Lithuania's literary circles was mixed, as even some seemingly intelligent critics could hardly cope with the challenge of Ričardas Gavelis. His narrative contained an inquiry into the essence of the oppressive totalitarian system and mysterious evil powers that are unnamed and only referred to as They. According to Gavelis, They had been conspiring against humans and attempting to fully control human societies since the times of Plato (and, in this sense, explicitly transcended one of its incarnations – the KGB). His narrative was so shocking and complex that most literary critics of the period were unable to deal with his themes.

Vilnius Poker was a very unusual novel, and not just in its attack upon the system that was gradually losing its grip on society as Lithuania's movement toward freedom progressed. It was truly shocking in various other aspects – not a single Lithuanian writer before Gavelis had dared to inquire into the essence of the oppressive system, not a single writer had dared to load his or her writings with sexually explicit themes and images (especially those of sexual violence), and no other writer had so openly and bravely discussed the Gulag experiences.

Moreover, Gavelis was the first Lithuanian fiction writer who set out to dissect its national mythology and attack the most sacred and venerated myths related to Lithuania's glory in the past. The novel was loaded with a quasi-philosophical, quasi-sociological discourse on *homo lithuanicus* – a type that, in Gavelis' eyes, was far more mean, chameleonic, and despicable than *homo sovieticus*. In addition, *Vilnius Poker* was probably the first openly post-modern Lithuanian novel that introduced a confusing and open-ended narrative (in fact, four different narratives told in the first-person by several characters, one of them being a dog), providing four different accounts of the events.

Vytautas Vargalys – the main protagonist of *Vilnius Poker* – is a highly ambiguous individual whose image of himself, however, contrasts with how other people view him, including those who are close to him and know him quite well. On the one hand, Vargalys is obsessed with finding out the whole truth about Them and uses his position (as a worker in a large state library) to collect any possible data about how They act and prey on their victims.

In this sense, his struggle might be interpreted as heroic, particularly since the quest for truth turns out to be life-threatening as They do not seem to be entertained by any idea of being followed or exposed. Martynas – Vytautas' friend and colleague, who works in the same library – is killed because, not being cautious enough, he opted to keep the study of Them on his computer. He failed to realize that They can easily break into any computer and destroy any evidence. Thus, Vytautas was far more aware of not trusting computers while secretly collecting evidence about these evil conspirators against humanity.

No matter how heroically Vytautas struggles to collect his evidence, he is hardly depicted as a true hero as he is revealed to be paranoid and overtly narcissistic at the same time. Vytautas feels far superior to any other human being in an intellectual sphere, and, last but not least, he describes himself as a sexual giant – something that turns out to be far from the truth according to other narratives (especially the one of Stefa, his lover/sexual slave). We also learn that while being interrogated by KGB operatives, Vytautas is subjected to horrendous torture, and his sexual organ is mutilated. Kelertas interprets him simultaneously as a hero who fights the basilisk of Vilnius and as a kind of anti-hero who humiliates other people, especially those who are closest to him (particularly Stefa). This kind of contradictory behavior and ambiguity in his character is inherently colonial and seen by Kelertas as something quite typical of a colonized individual:

> The colonial needs to feel superior even against all evidence to the contrary and it is especially significant, of course, that the area chosen for so-called achievement should be sexual, since colonized man is in many ways castrated, emasculated man. As has been noted by other scholars of postcolonialism, the postcolonial hero is often marked by a wound suggesting the tenuousness of his condition, the affliction brought on by colonialism, or as in Vytautas' case, the sadism of his torturers, as they brand two scars on his penis and according to some other versions in the novel leave him unable to reproduce his own kind, These are signs of colonial suffering, disfigurement, loss, infertility, and impotence. Vytautas, however, tries to deny his injury, physical and psychological, by compensating for his helplessness, degradation, and his lack of power by pretending to a superiority in the intellectual sphere.[7]

Kelertas goes on to speculate about the meaning encoded in Vytautas' name and finds certain associations with Lithuania's medieval ruler Vytautas the Great; a couple of interpretations of his surname Vargalys – 'the Copper-Ended' or 'the miserable' (*vargelis*) – contain some postcolonial connotations.[8] However, in my view, except for Copper-Ended (the term Gavelis himself uses in the text to explain the origin of the Vargalys family name), other interpretations are highly subjective as Vytautas was and continues to be one of the most popular Lithuanian names related to its historical figures and rulers. Notably, there are no hints in the text itself or in any available comments by Gavelis himself on his own novel pointing in this direction. On the other hand, I fully agree with Kelertas' judgment that *Vilnius Poker* is a genuinely postcolonial novel, and its main protagonist is an unmistakably postcolonial character struggling with his own self and fighting real as well as imagined demons in a society that can be described as colonial. However, the true meaning behind his activities is an attempt to convey the mystery of eternal supernatural power that appears disguised in different manners in different historical epochs.

Some literary scholars (including Kelertas) have labeled *Vilnius Poker* as the first truly postmodern Lithuanian novel, and critics have tended to agree with this judgment. Back in the 1990s, postmodernism was something that some literary scholars talked about but was beyond the radar of ordinary readers. However, most Lithuanian critics of the period only had a vague understanding of what postmodernism really meant because the majority lacked adequate knowledge about the most recent cultural and literary trends and their theoretical interpretations. Postmodernism was seen as a kind of ghost that existed somewhere in the West behind the Iron Curtain. For numerous reasons, this lack of understanding continued even after the fall of the Iron Curtain as Lithuanian literary scholars and critics suffered from their contact with the Western academic hemisphere and all its consequences.

Although Gavelis is very concerned with historical and mythological issues, he seems to suggest that there cannot be only one version of the events described in the book. Instead of one coherent narrative, he provides four. His translator Elizabeth Novickas, who discussed the novel even before she translated the book into English, observed the following:

> The world that Gavelis presents in his novel is even more complex; instead of two possible worlds, we get four; all of them presenting some overlap of events and characters, and all of them different. One is no more plausible than the other. Each narrator is equally flawed, each equally human (including the "Vox Candida"), each one's world colored and distorted by their own perceptions. There is no "true" version of events; instead, we are presented with the evidence that truth is only a relative quality, in the same way that time in the novel becomes a relative quality (Vargalys's and Stefa's narrations both take place on a single day – one consumes 244 pages, the other 42.)[9]

It has been suggested that Gavelis adopted the idea of different accounts of the same event that do not correspond with each other from *Rashomon*, an internationally acclaimed movie by Akira Kurosawa (based on short stories by Ryunosuke Akutagawa); his interest in this kind of narrative is revealed in his notebooks, which were handed over to the Institute of Lithuanian Literature and Folklore after his death.[10] This fact can also be confirmed by Gavelis' professional relationship with cinema: after giving up his career as an academic physicist, he spent some years working as a freelance scriptwriter for Lithuanian Film Studios and produced a number of scripts, though only a few were produced during the Soviet period.[11]

However, literary critics who are rediscovering the indebtedness of Gavelis' narrative to Akutagawa are, in fact, trying to reinvent the wheel, as the author of *Vilnius Poker* commented on this issue long ago. In his article "Anti-Demiurge, or What is *Vilnius Poker*," initially published in the weekly magazine *Literatūra ir menas* on April 21, 1990, and republished in *Bliuzas Ričardui Gaveliui* (Blues for Ričardas Gavelis), he thoroughly explained the narrative strategies behind the novel. In this highly important essay, Gavelis explained that "Akutagawa destroyed the demiurge with one well-aimed blow, a short story called *Thicket*. He understood one very simple thing: if you can't say 'it is so,' in literature, only 'I think so' can exist. The only natural way is to let all the participants of events speak, to show everyone's 'I think so.'"[12] In saying this, the author of *Vilnius Poker* was expressing how he no longer believed in any coherent storytelling by someone who supposedly knows everything as to how the story develops. Thus, as he explicitly explains in the essay, everything that happens in life might be described and interpreted in different or even a multitude of ways, as no one really knows for sure what or how things have happened. He goes on to explain his view by insisting, "Think for yourself: can we say that we 'know' anything in life? What in our world does it mean to say 'I know this'? Let's say that you 'know' everything about your friend. Where did all this knowledge come from? You saw his specific actions yourself, so you know this for sure? Ultimately, this is not true."[13]

Of course, this possibility of multiple versions threatens the general credibility of *Vilnius Poker*'s narrative as the reader can easily doubt whether any of the four versions provided is a *plausible* version of the events described. Are they all equally credible or equally incredible? Gavelis, in his musings about the demise of the traditional narrative and the need to introduce multiple narratives of the same story, however, does not go as far as to raise doubts about the dubiousness of the novel itself as it would have, most probably, killed not only the demiurge (which he dismissed in the essay mentioned above) but the trust of the potential reader as well.

Whatever it might be, the application of the principle of offering several versions of the same story provided *Vilnius Poker* with additional depth and mystery. On a certain level, this novel can be read as a detective story related to the mysterious death of Lolita – the object of Vytautas' love and passion. Nevertheless, the text does not provide any final clue, and the reader is left to solve the riddle for themselves. On the other hand, the novel is not about the murder of Lolita or any other character, for that matter. It is a dark, painful, and often uncomfortable novel about human suffering, injustice, and unfulfilled expectations, and many characters of *Vilnius Poker* die in one way or another. Thus, when reading the puzzle more deeply, who is responsible for Lolita's death becomes almost irrelevant.

One could also contemplate whether many readers choose to read *Vilnius Poker* as a murder mystery. In comparison to some other novels, for example, *The Name of the Rose* by Umberto Eco, the narrative(s) of *Vilnius Poker* is far less concentrated on solving the puzzle of Lolita's murder. She is just one of several characters who die under mysterious circumstances, and the author seems to imply that as long as the Soviet regime lasts, there will be no hope of either finding the truth or bringing any murderer to justice, as most of them are intricately connected with the violent mechanisms of the hidden regime. It is They – the mysterious timeless power that hides behind the institutions and has full control over people's lives – who decide who will be allowed to live and who will have to die.

Eternal Power and the Deadly Game

It is well-known that Gavelis wrote *Vilnius Poker* during a period when such an activity was not only dangerous for an author's literary career but could also easily affect the writer's fate by wiping him or her out of the literary discourse – or even worse. (As a matter of fact, books by his fellow prose writer Saulius Tomas Kondrotas were removed from public libraries after Kondrotas defected to the West. His titles immediately vanished from scholarly books and encyclopedias and remained absent until the collapse of the regime.) During the last two decades of the Soviet regime, dissidents and enemies of the state were rarely subjected to killings or torture; instead, more sophisticated means were developed to punish and silence those who sought to voice 'distortions' of the Soviet way of life: they were subjected to lengthy periods of imprisonment (in some cases, they were charged not only with political but also with criminal offenses) or isolated in psychiatric wards after undergoing compulsory psychiatric examination for prolonged periods. Needless to say, those who survived this kind of systemic torture were unable to find any skilled jobs or continue their professional careers after being released from such macabre institutions.

It is thus no surprise that a sinister novel containing an explicit critique of the regime and written in the Soviet era was kept hidden by several trusted friends of the author, who chose never to disclose their identities – even after the fall of the Soviet regime.

The reader is introduced to Them quite early in the development of the plot when Vytautas muses on being surveyed regularly by mysterious subjects that have no name:

> I've summoned *Them* again; once more I've given myself away, I've attracted attention. There can be no doubt: the shabby disa's stare, the unmistakable movements of her lips and cheeks were excessively clear… The horror is to know that it's as inevitable as the grass greening up in the spring, as the dragon's fiery breath. For a little while *They* stopped hiding and took aim at me again. My life is the life of a man in a telescopic sight. There would be nothing to it if the shotgun that is aimed at me would merely kill me. Alas… Who can understand this horrible condition, a condition I'm already accustomed to? Who can measure the depth of the drab abyss? The worst of it is that the trigger of that unseen shotgun is directly connected to you. Only you can pull it, so you have to be on your guard every moment, even when you are alone. Perhaps the most on guard when you're alone. Mere thoughts and desires, mere dreams, can give you away. *They* watch you, they watch you all the time and wait for you to make a mistake. With the second, true sight, I see the crooked smirk on *Their* plump faces, a smirk of faith in *Their* own unlimited power.[14]

Vytautas tries to comprehend the origins and power that these mysterious people possess. Inspired by Gediminas Riauba, his true mentor in his search for these powers who have ruled the world for more than two thousand years, he sets out to collect any available evidence of their existence. His obscure position and his duties at the library provide him with the perfect setting to pursue his goals. However, this pursuit is extremely dangerous, and he risks his own life to collect information on the subject of his studies. At a certain point, the protagonist admits that this endeavor requires exceptional strength and rigor. He even attempts to dismiss this highly troubling conspiracy theory:

> A hundred times I tried to logically refute *Their* existence. But I reached the opposite goal – I unarguably proved that *They* really exist. The simplest proof – an argument *ad absurdum*. Let's say *They* don't exist. There is no such subspecies of live creatures whose sole purpose is to kanuk people, to take away their intellectual and spiritual powers; that kingdom of sullen, flat faces doesn't exist. Let's say none of that exists.[15]

Nevertheless, Vytautas rejects this comfortable option of reasoning that could halt his further inquiry. He starts by analyzing the cases of his own century. He brings forward the evidence of the horrible atrocities committed by the likes of Stalin, Hitler, and Pol Pot and notes that most individuals from their respective societies denied or complied with the atrocities without attempting to prevent them. Moreover, he goes on to emphasize that even the most famous, most insightful, most respected philosophers throughout the history of mankind have never attempted to solve this horrible puzzle. He mentions a few exceptions, like Albert Camus, yet immediately observes that this French philosopher was at times *Their* apologist, as judged from his book *The Myth of Sisyphus*. However, he refuses to exclude Camus from the list of these exceptional thinkers, as some of his other writings (e.g., *The Plague*) allow Vytautas to think that such people as Camus or Franz Kafka are his co-conspirators and allies in his search for the truth about the existence of mysterious powers that have attempted to rule humanity since time immemorial. The protagonist cites the death of Camus as an irrefutable fact that They destroy individuals who set out to find out who they are and where they came from. But Vytautas still believes that despite their omnipotence, They can be traced, especially if one tracks them down methodically after conducting a detailed investigation:

> The fact that you won't find straightforward information about Them *in books ultimately proves* They *exist*. It would be easy to fight with a concrete societal or political organization that everyone knows or at least has come across. An identified enemy is *almost* a conquered enemy. Everyone would have risen up against *Them* a long time ago. *They* would have been destroyed at some point. Unfortunately, *Their* race exists and works harmoniously. But whether *They* want to or not, they leave traces behind. All of *Their* victims are indelible footprints.[16]

All this gives Vytautas some impetus to continue his investigation to unmask these mysterious yet powerful and deadly forces. His position in the library allows him to continue his ongoing search, though he has to take precautions so that none of his (mostly female) colleagues suspects him of crossing the borders of permissiveness.

Ultimately, it turns out that They are more powerful than anyone who believes they can trace them. Each and every protagonist in the novel who sets out to find out Their essence is destined to fail. Thus, the novel's implication is that the mysterious powers are far more powerful than any individual, even those who endow themselves with the mission of finding out the truth. Gediminas Riauba, Vytautas' hero, suffers a mysterious death and is eventually reborn in the form of a dog (the dog's narrative forms the fourth and final part of the novel). Martynas Poška, another conspirator against Them, dies after a large truck runs over him. Finally, Vargalys himself is accused of Lolita's murder and taken into custody, where he meets his death and posthumously reappears as one of the pigeons of Vilnius that he loathed while he was alive.

Thus, the search for the mysterious superpowers turns out to be a complete and irreversible defeat. No one, not even the most brave, insightful, and careful individual, is able to achieve their goal and unmask those evil powers that have conspired against humanity since time immemorial. Let us remember that when Gavelis was writing his novel (circa 1979–1987), Lithuania and the rest of the Baltic states were under the firm grip of the Soviet regime. Even if the system was slowly rotting on the inside, it seemed to go on forever, even after Mikhail Gorbachev's famous call for *perestroika*. In 1987, few, if any, could imagine that the system would finally collapse in just three years and Lithuania would be the first of its 'republics' to escape from the iron cage.

Some critics might be inclined to write off Gavelis' discourse on Them as merely another version of largely discredited conspiracy theories. However, any analysis focusing purely on conspiracy theories is, at best, a cursory attempt at understanding Gavelis' intentions. Instead of focusing exclusively on the Soviet secret service (the KGB) as the ultimate quintessence of power that rules a captive and colonized society, he has created a haunting metaphor for powers striving to subjugate and enslave entire societies over several millennia. Such an approach toward power makes his narrative more complex and adds considerable eeriness to the generally grim and macabre atmosphere of *Vilnius Poker*.

The Narrative's Sociological Digression:
Homo Lithuanicus

Nowhere in his novel does Ričardas Gavelis muse openly or, for that matter, conceptually about colonialism (the term is not even mentioned in the book). However, there are reflections upon the relations between the hegemonic power and the subaltern, between the colonizers and the colonized, throughout the text. On the other hand, it is no surprise that Gavelis uses different categories in *Vilnius Poker*, as colonialism was generally heavily exploited and even expropriated by the official ideology of the Soviet Union during the period when the novel was written. Official Soviet discourse claimed that colonialism was something that Western capitalist countries exclusively did to 'underdeveloped' nations, mainly in Africa and Asia. Thus, the USSR presented itself as an anti-colonial power and extended its 'help' to African and Asian countries facing issues during the process of decolonization. This also explains why one can only find a few references, if any, to colonialism in Lithuanian fiction from the Soviet period.

Nevertheless, Gavelis dealt with the issue of colonialism and was deeply concerned as to what happens to human beings when individuals become the subjects of a society where each and every freedom is denied by the ruling regime. Curiously, while contemplating the fate of his colonized nation, the author introduced quasi-philosophical and quasi-sociological insertions into his seemingly purely fictional text. Though Gavelis is hardly known for mixing genres, his digression into a non-fiction narrative is essential to the whole structure of *Vilnius Poker*.

Musings on *homo sovieticus* and his close (as well as more appalling) relative, *homo lithuanicus*, appear in the third part of the book, narrated by Martynas Poška. While contemplating various issues of his environment, Martynas attempts to grasp the difference between the two apparently close notions. In the form of a monologue, he speculates as follows:

> For the thousandth time, listening to the divine Elena, I thought about whether *homo lithuanicus* really differs all that much from *homo sovieticus*: is it permissible to consider the former a separate anthropomorphous species, or is it merely a subspecies of the latter? Once more I decide it's permissible. *Homo lithuanicus* has characteristics that are absolutely atypical of the species *homo sovieticus*. *Homo lithuanicus* says "they," *homo sovieticus* says "we." *Homo lithuanicus* considers only Lithuania his country. To him the remaining parts of the USSR are as distant and as foreign as Mars. *Homo sovieticus* considers the entire USSR his home country. Just look at the Russians living in Vilnius or Tbilisi. They feel at home, in their own place; from their point of view, all these Lithuanians and Georgians aren't quite where they belong. *Homo sovieticus* doesn't sense any difference between Mogilyov, Ryazan, or Dnipropetrovs'k. (And by the way, there is none.) According to *homo lithuanicus*' understanding, Vilnius is as different from Saratov as the sky from the earth.[17]

The excerpt, though hinting at certain irreconcilable differences between the two types, provides characteristics of *homo lithuanicus* that are hardly flattering. Though the digression from the infamous conceptualization of *homo sovieticus* might imply that his 'junior brother' is more sympathetic, this is not the case, as is made evident when Gavelis unfolds the theme via Martynas' philosophizing on the unique qualities of both social types. It turns out that, in comparison with his older and senior relative, there is nothing in any way superior about *homo lithuanicus*.

Later in the text, going from one subject to another, Martynas once again compares the two social types. The reader soon learns that some of the supposed advantages of this junior relative in fact conceal an even uglier, even more deplorable type as *homo lithuanicus* fails to meet even the bleakest standards of the infamous *homo sovieticus*. Without referring directly to this type, the narrator provides an account of a situation on public transport where a mother is being questioned innocently by her young son. When, after being told that Lithuanians live in Lithuania, French in France, and Americans in America, he continues to ask his mother why so many Russians live in Lithuania, she is both perplexed and horrified by the question. Moreover, instead of admitting that the boy exhibits some qualities of common sense, she dismisses the question as impossible, believing that some malicious people have brainwashed her child. The narrator describes her as a convert. She has been converted to the ideology imposed on her by the colonizers and no longer distinguishes between words and their true meaning.

Though *homo lithuanicus* often feels superior to his older relative, *homo sovieticus*, Martynas eventually shatters this naïve and essentially deceptive illusion. While musing on the subject, the narrator observes that public toilets, which he describes as the last remaining shelters of relative freedom in this system of total control, sometimes contain graffiti (and these profane, vulgar writings express some truths about the nature of society and the ruling regime). However, even this poor graffiti is only done in Russian. Thus, the narrator argues that *homo lithuanicus* – a humble and obedient sort, ready to serve his colonizers in any situation and at any cost – is unable to express himself even in the solitude of a lavatory stall. In this sense, he is far inferior to *homo sovieticus* as the latter still believes that something might be said to power. Yet *homo lithuanicus* is incapable even of allowing himself to think that situation can be altered, reversed, or resisted in any way. Moreover, he fully and irrevocably conforms to the situation of being colonized: "*Homo lithuanicus*, unable to express himself freely, would rather carry his soul to the grave without it ever being put to use. That's how nations die."[18] Elsewhere in his narrative, Martynas says that "*Homo lithuanicus*, unfortunately, realized only too well that to lose is very easy and comfortable. Then you can blame everything in the world – just not yourself. Lord knows, it's really comfortable. And gratefully, elegantly sad. *Homo lithuanicus* tends to do nothing but feel sorry for himself and bemoan his melancholy end."[19]

There is no doubt that precisely this kind of characterization of Lithuanian society and its individuals, who were brought up under the conditions of long-term subservience and colonization, caused indignation

and even fury among some readers and a considerable number of literary
critics. Such an approach to *homo lithuanicus* was in many cases taken as
extremely offensive. In fact, Gavelis posed a serious, almost unheard-of
challenge to his society by debunking national mythology, false self-
imaging, and one-sided, albeit often heroic, interpretations of Lithuania's
history and pre-colonial past. He adopted a cold, rational (some would even
say cynical), analytical, sociologically neutral attitude toward the captive
society, the members of which sought to justify their passivity, conformity,
and obedience as a kind of literary mirror, revealing the ugly truth about the
captives themselves. The refusal to treat individuals of a Sovietized society
exclusively as victims of a foreign power, together with uncompromising
insights into the characteristics of the national character, was a serious
violation of the unwritten literary taboos of the Soviet era. These taboos
were inflicted upon the cultural consciousness not by the power structures
of the Soviet regime but by the captive society itself. Until the arrival of
Vilnius Poker, society was essentially comfortable seeing itself as an
innocent victim of historical circumstances and larger neighboring powers.
Accordingly, it was always the Other who was responsible for the flawed
developments of Lithuania's history.

In the novel, Gavelis shares his ideas about his fellow Lithuanian writers
(and, more generally, intellectuals of the colonial period) through Martynas
while he is talking to his female colleagues. The image of the writer he
mediates is neither comforting nor justifying; instead, his diagnosis of
Soviet Lithuanian *literati* is sober and no less ruthless. He sees them as
nothing more and nothing less than the true incarnation of *homo lithuanicus*,
illustrating this through Martynas, who characterizes a typical Lithuanian
writer:

> every seven years a creative fever overcomes him. The symptoms: muses
> and ghosts torment him. His entire body starts itching. The pain is horrible.
> The time has come to beg the authorities for a new apartment. There aren't
> many apartments, but writers multiply like dogs. That's when the
> Shakespearean passions boil over. Sung in tones of the highest spirituality.
> What eloquence! What depth! You see at once that these are artists. What
> Greek tragedies! The Soviet writer could kill his brother and sister over a
> new apartment, or still worse – he could kill himself! I know at least six
> writers who publicly threatened suicide if the state wouldn't give them a new
> apartment.[20]

These observations suggest that the whole society is sick. Even those writers
and intellectuals who aspire to be society's extraordinary spiritual leaders
are nothing but ordinary submissive individuals trying to negotiate as many

goods and favors as possible from the authorities they hate with all their hearts. This ambiguity and hypocrisy are inevitable features of a captive society deprived of the right to govern itself.

The Self and Beyond: From Stigma to Postcolonial Subject

In her article "Perceptions of the Self and the Other in Lithuanian Postcolonial Fiction," Violeta Kelertas sought to discuss the complex and often contradictory character of Vytautas Vargalys. I share her observation that Vytautas – or, for that matter, the majority of the protagonists of the Vilnius trilogy (made up of *Vilnius Poker*, *Vilnius Jazz*, and *The Last Generation of People on Earth*) – might be well classified as truly postcolonial.

Unlike other Lithuanian fiction writers who maintained a critical attitude toward the communist regime and its ideology, Gavelis refused to have a rosy attitude toward pre-Soviet Lithuanian society. Vytautas, like other characters in *Vilnius Poker* like Gediminas Riauba or Martynas Poška, refuse to glorify Lithuania's past, and they even find parts of it ridiculous. Respectful attitudes toward national symbols and values (Gediminas' Tower, the Iron Wolf, etc.) give way to merciless criticism of the national character and reflections on the origin of Lithuanian's passivity and tendency to conform with those who are aggressive and have more power. Episodes from the country's history are reflected upon without romanticism and exaltation. The concept of a glorious, heroic past is cast aside, and Lithuanians are blamed for submitting themselves to foreign powers, especially Russia and, eventually, the Soviet Union.

On the other hand, none of the main characters of *Vilnius Poker* aspires to exemplify any heroic traits of their character. Even those who consciously distance themselves from the regime, resist its impact on the habits of thinking and acting (like Vytautas, Gediminas, or Martynas), and engage in certain kinds of subversive activities (or at least believe that their inquiry into Them is highly subversive) often exhibit the moral ambiguity of their character. For example, Vytautas and his mentor Gediminas share misogynist attitudes toward women. Both of them indulge in morally dubious activities, like occasional sexual orgies. Vytautas' relationship with Stefa, whom he habitually uses to satisfy his sexual desires while remaining attracted to his main love interest, Lolita, and especially his attitude toward his 'sexual slave,' remain morally ambiguous, to say the least.

Gediminas' and Vytautas' common love interest, Lolita, is an equally complex and ambiguous character. Being the daughter of a repulsive, cruel, and cynical KGB colonel, her motives for having sexual relationships with both protagonists might be well interpreted as somewhat ambiguous. Moreover, both Gediminas and Vytautas share not only a passion for her but also an interest in researching the mysterious powers ruling their society (and the whole of mankind). Furthermore, at some point, it is hinted that Lolita might be responsible for Gediminas' untimely and violent death. Later in the novel, Vytautas is framed for Lolita's murder. However, it is difficult to avoid the suspicion (hinted at elsewhere in the text) that he is not just an innocent victim who was chosen and framed by the KGB in order to compromise him but that he might indeed be directly involved in Lolita's gruesome death.

While musing on the postcolonial aspects of *Vilnius Poker* and other novels by Gavelis, Kelertas draws attention to the fates of all the most important male characters of *Vilnius Poker* who ultimately fail to achieve their ambitious goals:

> One of the main points that VV's version demonstrates is that the colonial needs to hang to his dignity by lying to himself about his superiority vis-à-vis the enemy. He needs to have a project to occupy himself and delude himself into thinking that he is accomplishing something by observing and classifying the enemy. He thinks this gives him power over the enemy, but in reality he has absolutely no power because the weak at least survive, while the strong, like the three "thinking" types that we are given access to, are all destroyed. VV is framed into killing Lolita, the thing he loved, or at least is accused of it, dies and is turned into a pigeon, leaving the KGB headquarters in this form (he always hated pigeons with their blank stare): Riauba either dies in a car crash or is drowned by Lolita whom he also loved and made love to, and is turned into a dog until the next accident will end his current afterlife; Martynas is run over by a truck and no doubt is also one of the ubiquitous Vilnius pigeons or crows or sparrows. So died Camus and many others, asserts Gavelis, because they knew too much.[21]

Throughout the novel, Gavelis offers different and contradicting versions of the events described as well as conflicting accounts of what his characters think about themselves and how other individuals see them. For example, Vytautas boasts of his sexual prowess and even refers to his family name (Vargalys – 'the Copper-Ended') to support his image of the self. However, this narrative is contradicted by the accounts of at least two female characters – Stefa and Lolita – who attest that his male organ was badly hurt during KGB interrogations. (Vytautas himself recalls the episode when his sadistic interrogator suggested that his equally sadistic fellow officer used fire to mutilate his penis.) Incidentally, Gavelis regularly uses allusions to bodily suffering and pain in *Vilnius Poker* as well as in his other writings.

For example, his short story *Handless* tells the grisly tale of a Lithuanian Gulag prisoner who agrees to have his hand chopped off while escaping the prison in order to send a message to the outer world while he and his fellow prisoners remain imprisoned in the unbearable cold and the snowfields.[22]

The former prisoner of a Soviet Gulag who has survived the unbearable conditions of forced labor in Siberia and returned to his home country is a recurrent character in Gavelis' novels and short stories. This is hardly surprising because a large number of Lithuanians were deported to various places across the Soviet Union immediately after the Red Army re-entered the country at the end of World War II. In fact, entire families, including children and the elderly, were packed off and sent to Siberia and elsewhere in railway wagons originally intended to transport livestock. Many died of thirst, hunger, or exhaustion before reaching their final destination. Those who had been directly involved in anti-Soviet activities or armed resistance were either killed or sentenced to long-term imprisonment in the Gulags. Needless to say, many did not see the end of their imprisonment, and some of those who managed to endure the harsh climate and inhuman conditions of confinement and forced labor returned home in poor health and with various bodily injuries inflicted upon them during their imprisonment.

For several decades after the war, Lithuanian writers were discouraged from discussing these experiences as even the mildest freedom of expression was strictly controlled by the censorship authorities. Those who trespassed the boundaries of what was allowed were threatened with severe consequences. These bans temporarily decreased during the so-called Khrushchev Thaw, when Stalinist policies were subjected to an element of scrutiny and criticism. Some (but only some) inmates of Gulags could return home without serving their entire prison term. Censorship continued to exist until the re-establishment of Lithuania's independence, and during the last decade of the Soviet regime, it became less rigid.[23] Nevertheless, many Lithuanian writers continued to avoid these dangerous issues, and those who referred to deportations and Siberian exile did this at the risk of their literary careers – and more.

Gavelis, however, did not shy away from these potentially dangerous themes early in his career. His short-story collection *Nubaustieji* (The Punished, 1987), published before Gorbachev's *perestroika* took hold in Lithuania, contains depictions of and reflections on deportations as well as important insights into Gulag experiences. And yet, prose writers had to be very careful when dealing with these issues. Any open discussions about how Lithuania lost its independence and fell under the rule of the Soviet Union were taboo for several decades after the war. As Gavelis evidently had no expectations for *Vilnius Poker* to be published in Lithuania during the period when he wrote it (as mentioned earlier, the manuscript was divided into several parts and kept by a few of his most reliable friends), he was able to discuss the issue of the Gulags without any restrictions of censorship, whether this was imposed by the authorities or through the widespread practice of self-censorship.

Individuals who were deported to Siberia and elsewhere during the Soviet period, especially those imprisoned in the Gulag system for any kind of anti-Soviet activities, can be treated as a stigmatized social group. Many of them were not allowed to return to Lithuania after serving their sentence and were confined to other republics of the Soviet Union. Even after finally coming back to their home country, they remained under surveillance. As former political prisoners, they were regularly summoned to the KGB for interviews, and their job possibilities were restricted. Thus, individuals with such experiences usually preferred to keep silent about their past and shared their stories only with people who had suffered the same fate.

Sociologist Erving Goffman has analyzed various aspects and manifestations of stigmatized individuals and discussed how stigma affects the making of personal identity. According to Goffman,

> For the individual to have had what is called a shady past is an issue regarding his social identity; the way he handles information about this past is a question of personal identification. Possession of a strange past (not strange in itself, of course, but strange for someone of the individual's current social identity) is one kind of impropriety; for the possessor to live out a life before those who are ignorant of this past and not informed about it by him can be a very different kind of impropriety, the first having to do with our rules regarding social identity, the second with those regarding personal identity.[24]

Goffman claims that the discrepancy between what he calls "virtual and actual identity"[25] strongly affects an individual's social identity, and thus a stigmatized person will most likely feel distant or even be hostile to a society of which he is a member. His real past, which is different from the personal histories of other individuals, can (and often do) make him feel strange, isolated, and even desolate. The way Vytautas Vargalys skillfully hides his Gulag experience and, thus, this attitude confirms that, psychologically, he can be seen as a stigmatized individual with a broken personal identity that he is unable to heal under the prevailing regime. Any integrity of personhood is impossible as the ruling regime and its institutions pursue policies that enforce only those attitudes that consolidate stigmatization. On the other hand, under the conditions of oppression, the stigma of an individual who has a different past is sustained by the so-called 'normal' members of the colonized society who avoid such experiences and generally keep a distance from those individuals who are supposed to have deviated from the approved 'normalcy.'

This 'strangeness' of Vytautas' biography makes him insecure in the company of his library colleagues, who lack his past experience. They do not know or even suspect that he was once a prisoner of a Gulag for his activities against the regime. Thus, he feels more at home with a few friends and acquaintances who, like him, once spent some time in a similar location or who, like him, do not feel at home with the rules and limits set by the regime. The identification of his personhood is not with members of his society but rather with a few exceptional individuals who share his experiences or feelings toward the system that caused these experiences. As Albert Memmi emphasized in his well-known book *The Colonizer and the Colonized*,

> As long as he tolerates colonization, the only possible alternatives for the colonized are assimilation or petrification. Assimilation being refused him, as we shall see, nothing is left for him but to live isolated from his age. He is driven back by colonization and, to a certain extent, lives with that situation. Planning and building his future are forbidden. He must therefore limit himself to the present, and even that present is cut off and abstract.[26]

Vytautas realizes that he has to hide his true 'self' in order to survive, particularly since he is aware of being regularly observed. On the other hand, he refuses to trust anyone as he believes any individual might be following him under Their orders. He contemplates the necessity of having a person with whom he can share his views and pass on certain tasks, but he immediately concedes that such a trustworthy individual does not exist:

> I needed an assistant, a person I could depend on. Martynas wasn't suitable, he was too intelligent and too curious. I was completely sick of Stefa 'accidentally' getting under foot all the time, but she had already served her purpose. I needed a person who would help without asking too many questions, whom I could satisfy with vague stories about a dissertation or a scholarly work. Vilnius didn't want to give me that kind of person.[27]

Thus the protagonist of the novel remains lonely and isolated. Loneliness, isolation, and strangeness are the constant features of his personal identity. Being unable to trust anybody, even for a good reason, Vytautas is destined to remain isolated forever, despite being closely attached to a few individuals like Gediminas or Martynas, who share his views but have different personal histories. There is no doubt that Vytautas is an extremely complex character as his personal identity is formed in association with his stigma as a former Gulag prisoner who remains a suspect in both the eyes of a colonized society and its institutions that control the behavior of its individuals. Vytautas naturally exhibits certain characteristics that make him feel significantly different from others and, accordingly, lonely and isolated. He feels different from other members of society, partially because of his past, which distinguishes him from his fellow citizens. This explains why he exaggerates his personality and puts himself into the center of events even though he is often no more than a passive observer, such as when Mikhail Suslov visits Vilnius – we learn from the text that he was supposed to kill the infamous Communist Party functionary.

Images of disability are closely related to Gavelis' characters not only in *Vilnius Poker* but in his other writings as well. For example, the protagonist of his short story *Handless* loses his hand. He gives this part of his body voluntarily during the breakout from a Siberian Gulag when he and his friends are trapped in the icy snow on the bank of the river and are trying to determine how they can send a message to the outer world about their existence. As the story progresses, we learn that the protagonist's family name and the sacrifice of his hand to save himself and the others are not accidental: all his male family members have lost their hands (or arms) during their lifetimes. Vytautas Vargalys is not represented as a disabled person, but his self-image (he regularly boasts of his sexual prowess) contradicts the accounts provided by other characters (especially women with whom he had amorous or sexual relations). By comparing the different accounts provided by male and female characters of *Vilnius Poker*, the reader gradually comes to realize that Vytautas is quite possibly hiding and masking his sexual disability (or at least lack of male power) by providing a misleading narrative on his inexhaustible and super-human sexual organ (and power). These motifs of physical disability are characteristic of postcolonial writings. As Ato Quayson has suggested,

> The presence of disabled people in postcolonial writing marks more than just the recognition of their obvious presence in the real worlds of postcolonial existence and the fact that in most cases national economies woefully fail to take care of them. It means much more than that. It also marks the sense of a major problematic, which is nothing less than the difficult encounter with history itself. For colonialism may be said to have been a major force of disabling the colonized from taking their place in the flow of history other than in a position of stigmatized underprivilege.[28]

It is difficult to prove whether Gavelis consciously created images of disability in his novels and short stories as allusions to the powerlessness of the colonized individuals and societies. However, the fact that disabled characters regularly occur in his writings indicates that these images were hardly accidental. By contrasting power (or the lack of it) with images of disabled male characters who belong to the subjugated and the colonized, Gavelis might have been attempting to imply something much more than just referring to the physical traits of certain characters.

There is one more feature of *Vilnius Poker* that needs to be considered. A close reading of the novel shows that Gavelis creates characters who can hardly be called 'heroes,' as they all are extremely complex and often contradictory. The interpretation of *Vilnius Poker* as a postcolonial novel allows one to understand why the author created characters who do not really fall into the category of 'positive' or 'heroic.' Like the characters of the Hollywood movie *Crash*, the protagonists of *Vilnius Poker* might act as heroes in one episode and anti-heroes or even repulsive characters in another. What the author seems to suggest with this kind of attitude toward his characters is that a colonial regime based on structural violence, submission, and coercion does not create any heroes, even among those who wholeheartedly oppose it. Moreover, any attempts to grasp the origins of the power that rules society under various guises (totalitarianism is one of the incarnations of eternal and total power) and the methods They apply to control and manipulate people are ultimately doomed.

Needless to say, this implication is alarming, even though the text is a work of fiction. This is only one of the reasons why reading *Vilnius Poker* is in no way light entertainment and cannot aspire to being a work of fiction that provides emotional balance and peace of heart. The novel does not provide simple answers but rather raises a lot of uncomfortable and often upsetting questions. The very structure of the novel, which gives four completely different narrative versions of the same events, implies that no one can claim to know the whole truth about anything described in *Vilnius Poker*.

Notes

[1] Samalavičius, "Ričardas Gavelis."
[2] Tamošaitis, "Literatūra ant debesies."
[2] Jonušys, "Prozos proveržiai."
[3] Kubilius, "Bjaurumo estetikos paribiuose."
[4] Jonušys, "Prozos proveržiai," 1.
[5] See Kerletas, ed., *Baltic Postcolonialism.*
[6] Čerškutė, "Nerandu kito tokio kūrėjo kaip Ričardas Gavelis."
[7] Kelertas, "Perceptions of the Self and the Other," 254.
[8] Ibid, 253.
[9] Novickas, "Delving the Nightmare of Ričardas Gavelis' 'Vilniaus Pokeris," 55.

[10] Čerškutė, "Vilniaus pokeris," 81–100
[11] Čerškutė, Ibid.
[12] Gavelienė et al., eds., *Bliuzas Ričardui Gaveliui.*
[13] Ibid, 183.
[14] Gavelis, *Vilnius Poker*, 8–9.
[15] Ibid, 57.
[16] Ibid, 60.
[17] Ibid, 334.
[18] Ibid, 365.
[19] Ibid.
[20] Ibid, 75–76.
[21] Kelertas, "Perceptions of the Self and the Other," 257–258.
[22] A more detailed discussion on Gavelis' use of bodily images and metaphors can be found in Samalavičius, "Lithuanian Prose and Decolonisation," 409–427.
[23] For an overview of how censorship was institutionalized in the Soviet era and how it eventually changed, see Samalavičius, "Lithuania."
[24] Goffman, "Stigma," 64.
[25] Ibid, 19.
[26] Memmi, *The Colonizer and the Colonized*, 102.
[27] Gavelis, *Vilnius Poker*, 202.
[28] Quayson, "Looking Awry," 228.

Works Cited

Čerškutė, Jūratė. "Nerandu kito tokio kūrėjo kaip Ričardas Gavelis." *Apzvalga.* https://www.apzvalga.eu/jurate-cerskute-nerandu-kito-tokio-kurejo-kaip-ricardas-gavelis.html (accessed May 27, 2019).

—. "'Vilniaus pokeris': nuo rašiomono iki dekonstrukcinio pasakojimo." *Colloquia* 29 (2013): 81–100.

Gavelienė, Nijolė, Antanas A. Jonynas, and Almantas Samalavičius, eds. *Bliuzas Ričardui Gaveliui: atsiminimai, užrašai paraštėse, laiškai, eseistika, kūrybos analizė.* Vilnius: Tyto alba, 2007.

Gavelis, Ričardas. *Vilnius Poker.* Translated by Elizabeth Novickas. Rochester, NY: Open Letter, 2009.

Goffman, Erving. *Stigma: Notes on the Management of Spoiled Identity.* New York: Simon and Schuster, 1963.

Jonušys, Laimantas. "Prozos proveržiai." *15min.lt.* https://www.15min.lt/kultura/naujiena/literatura/laimantas-jonusys-prozos-proverziai-286-297523 (accessed May 27, 2019).

Kelertas, Violeta. *Baltic Postcolonialism.* Amsterdam/New York: Rodopi, 2006.

—. "Perceptions of the Self and the Other in Lithuanian Postcolonial Fiction." In *Baltic Postcolonialism*, edited by Violeta Kelertas, 251–269. Amsterdam/New York: Rodopi, 2006.

Kubilius, Vytautas. "Bjaurumo estetikos paribiuose." *metai* 12 (2002). https://www.zurnalasmetai.lt/?p=6871.

Memmi, Albert. *The Colonizer and the Colonized*. New York: Grove Press, 1960.

Novickas, Elizabeth. "Delving the Nightmare of Ričardas Gavelis' 'Vilniaus Pokeris'." *Lituanus* 50, no. 3 (2004). http://www.lituanus.org/2004/04_3_5Novickas.htm.

Quayson, Ato. "Looking Awry: Tropes of Disability in Postcolonial Writing," In *Relocating Postcolonialism*, edited by David Theo Goldberg and Ato Quayson, 217–230. Oxford: Blackwell, 2002.

Samalavičius, Almantas. "Lithuania." In *Censorship: An International Encyclopedia*. London: Fitzroy Dearborn Publishers, 2001.

—. "Lithuanian Prose and Decolonisation: Rediscovery of the Body." In *Baltic Postcolonialism*, edited by Violeta Kelertas, 409–428. Amsterdam/New York: Rodopi, 2006.

—. "Ričardas Gavelis." In *Dictionary of Literary Biography*, vol. 353: *Twenty-First-Century Central and Eastern European Writers*, edited by Steven Serafin and Vasa D. Mihailovich, 81–84. New York: Gale, 2010.

Tamošaitis, Regimantas. "Literatūra ant debesies." *Bernardinai.lt*, July 25, 2013. https://www.bernardinai.lt/2013-07-25-literatura-ant-debesies/.

CHAPTER III

LETTERS FROM THE PAST:
MEMOIRS OF A LIFE CUT SHORT
BY RIČARDAS GAVELIS

As I have already emphasized, Ričardas Gavelis was one of the most important (if not *the* most important) Lithuanian prose writers of the last Soviet decades and the early post-Soviet period. He shook the Lithuanian cultural establishment with an early novel that turned out to be his *magnum opus – Vilnius Poker*, which first appeared in 1989 and, quite unusually for the literary culture of the late Soviet period, was followed by a second edition just a year later. Being a somewhat established and relatively well-known young writer and author of several collections of short stories that were well-received by readers and literary critics alike, as well as a playwright with several staged theater productions (as well as a film script) to his credit, Gavelis immediately rose to literary stardom after the publication of *Vilnius Poker*, which was discussed in the preceding chapter and other publications.[1] His early fame and popularity (or even stardom), however, turned out to be both a blessing and a curse.

Although Gavelis became the most widely read Lithuanian writer and a media celebrity, constantly interviewed in daily papers and appearing on TV as well as receiving several dozen book reviews, it soon became apparent that he was destined to remain an isolated literary loner envied and even despised by some of his fellow Lithuanian writers, who felt (and in fact were) overshadowed by his instant fame. At the same time, he was misunderstood or ignored by academic critics, who seemed to be totally unable to find any key to interpret his writings.

From the current perspective, the reasons for this cold, if not hostile, attitude are quite obvious: neither the literary nor the popular audience was ready to meet the powerful challenges of *Vilnius Poker*'s imagery: representations of Lithuania's capital as the 'ass of the universe,' a penetrating and demystifying quasi-philosophical and sociological discourse on *homo lithuanicus* (a human type that he found even more morally corrupt than his twin brother, *homo sovieticus*), attacks on semi-sacred national symbols like Gediminas' Tower (referred to in the novel as a 'blunt phallus'), satirizing the loss of national pride and submissive obedience to the Soviet colonizers, and so forth. After being invited to give a graduate seminar on Lithuanian contemporary literature and criticism at Vilnius University back in 1998, I was surprised to find out that several dozen graduate students of Lithuanian literature viewed him as little more than a pop writer obsessed with pornographic images. It took quite an effort to convince them that *Vilnius Poker* did not fall into typical categories.

Today, all this seems risible as the reception of his literary work changed significantly after his premature death. Despite never being given any significant literary prize in his lifetime, Gavelis is now widely read by new generations of Lithuanians, and many of his books – both collections of short stories and novels – have been republished and reprinted, though none had as large a circulation as *Vilnius Poker.*

The Colonial Narrative

Jauno žmogaus memuarai (Memoirs of a Life Cut Short), a shorter but no less mature and impressive novel than *Vilnius Poker*, was translated into English by Jayde Will and published in the United Kingdom in 2018. The origins of *Memoirs of a Life Cut Short* are still clouded by the same secrecy as *Vilnius Poker*. Most likely, no one will ever learn where the author kept his manuscript before it was eventually published. Both novels were started and finished years before they could be published both were kept hidden by close friends he could trust, and he never indicated their names even two decades after their publication. *Memoirs of a Life Cut Short* was published in book form in 1991, but the novel was already well-known to the literary audience since it was published in a series form in 1989 by Lithuania's largest literary monthly magazine, *Pergalė* (presently known as *Metai*). Thus, *Vilnius Poker* and *Memoirs of a Life Cut Short* were actually published in the same year – 1989 – before the collapse of the Soviet regime in Lithuania.

As mentioned above, both books were written during a period when the author had no chance of seeing them published; they were supposed to stay 'in the drawers' until some hard-to-foresee time when state censorship would cease to be as rigid as it was in Leonid Brezhnev's era. Significant changes took place after Mikhail Gorbachev's call for reforms and the Lithuanian movement for implementing *perestroika* (which eventually became the national resurgence movement) got into full swing. Because of these socio-political developments, the publication of both novels became possible.

Memoirs of a Life Cut Short is beyond any doubt one of the best novels ever written by Ričardas Gavelis, who penned seven books in this genre in addition to several collections of short stories and occasional essays. The novel is focused on the life story (no matter how brief) of its protagonist, Levas Ciparis. Levas is a young man who grew up in the poisonous atmosphere of the late Soviet era when the regime of Leonid Brezhnev became famous for its cynicism, corruption, and hypocrisy, known as the 'stagnation period.' In a certain sense, this is Gavelis' version of a traditional *Bildungsroman*; however, coming of age in the context of the Soviet era is interpreted as anything but natural or, for that matter, easy. The protagonist reflects upon his childhood, adolescence, and coming of age from a post-mortem perspective while at the same time presenting a brilliant literary autopsy of the Soviet regime before it was finally dismantled. Its narrative is constructed in the form of fourteen letters that Levas writes to his spiritual mentor and physics student, Tomas Kelertas (a character who regularly appears in many of Gavelis' other writings). Though Levas and Tomas are close friends, they represent quite different personalities: Levas is very sensitive and emotional, while Tomas is more rational and exercises common sense.

This series of private letters reveal the hidden mechanisms of the 'Empire of Evil,' as the Soviet Union was famously called by President Ronald Reagan. Through his employment of the old genre of letter writing (though the letters are not dated), the protagonist reveals his own creeping moral decay in the milieu of a culture based on lies and hypocrisy. These memoirs also include shorter letters addressed to a number of renowned writers and intellectuals of the last century like Franz Kafka, Albert Camus, Jose Ortega y Gasset, the renowned Lithuanian author Vincas Mykolaitis-Putinas, and the notorious leader of the Soviet Union himself, Leonid Brezhnev.

One of the main issues with which Gavelis is preoccupied in this early novel (like in all other writings of this genre) is the question of power, or more accurately, how power affects people who have it, those who aspire to it, and those who remain subject to it. As a writer, Gavelis is interested in how power originates, what forms it takes, and especially, what impact it has upon individuals and their fates. On the other hand, his search for answers is located in a particular time and space: Lithuania in the late Soviet era, when many illusions and hopes no longer exist, when the colonial system seems to last forever.

However, when analyzing people's attraction to and seduction by power in *Memoirs of a Life Cut Short*, Gavelis does not speak of power in terms of They – a hauntingly perceptive image he elaborated in his *magnum opus*,

Vilnius Poker. In this shorter novel (written almost simultaneously with his longer one), Gavelis bypasses sociological discourse focused on Them and chooses other images of 'the great community' (the almighty Communist Party) and its ideological tool, termed 'phantasmagorical spores.' These are the reflexive concepts with the help of which Gavelis dissects the double-faced promising Soviet physicist and examines how one transforms oneself into the system's faithful and obedient servant. The latter choice, as proved by the example of the short life span of Levas Ciparis, results in a conscious disposal of one's true self, which eventually leads to the road toward degradation and self-destruction.

To pursue his professional and social career, Levas has no other option but to join the Komsomol and climb the ladder of this junior communist league. At least, he cannot imagine any other way to pursue his goals. However, his decision is not taken lightly, and he attempts to explain it in one of his letters to Tomas:

> You, of course, are secretly mocking me, even though you are trying to keep a serious facial expression. Oh, I didn'tl want to associate with those "internal emigrants,' but getting involved with the Komsomol apparatus was just the thing for me? I understand your derision, Tomas, because you were one of the few real emigrants, without any quotation marks. But understand me too. I wanted to live and do something. Maybe I didn't exactly choose my path; it's more likely it had already been chosen for me. Now when the plugs has been taken out of many people's mouths, everyone – mostly those whose mouths were never plugged – suddenly became wise and *en masse* began to see again. The Komsomol is a formal organisation, the Komsomol apparatus is a breeding ground for bureaucrats, and so on and so forth. They are all clever, they understand everything so well that it's even scary. I already understood a lot back then, I felt the overwhelming power of the horrible spores, but at least I'm honest and admit that I didn't have any big objections to it. We all – yes, yes, all of us! were so stuck to the idea that the status quo was totally unshakeable, that we didn't pay attention to the endless nonsense. I also didn't pay attention to it, like everyone else. I simply tried to at least do something, at least achieve something.[2]

The Embodiment of Power

Gavelis includes a third element into this seemingly bipolar system (of Levas vs. Tomas) through the image of a father-in-law, who epitomizes those embedded in power and become its eternal agents. However, Levas' father-in-law is presented as much more than a wise, cunning, and morally corrupt Soviet bureaucrat. In fact, he is a member of the elite Communist

Party club, and he is also a strategist of its policy and a philosopher who gives meaning to that policy and any actions of the authorities.

It is this horrifying character, or even perhaps an elaborate concept/paradigm of a person, who acts as a direct link to those conspirators against humanity who have sought to control humans since the times of Plato that are so thoughtfully, insightfully, and provocatively discussed by Gavelis in *Vilnius Poker*. Moreover, the father-in-law in *Memoirs of a Life Cut Short* is perhaps one of the most disturbing characters ever created by Gavelis. He is much more than a standard Soviet bureaucrat performing his duties, more than a 'gray' representative of its power structures, and does not represent the 'banality of evil' discussed by Hannah Arendt. In essence, he is an embodiment of evil who is conscious of his motives and deeds and recognizes no moral thresholds on his path. This self-confident character makes one's skin crawl: he is clever, calm, well-balanced, and cynical, yet absolutely devoted to his cause. He is not afraid of any social or political changes or, for that matter, even the regime's demolition. He knows perfectly well that the power he represents will remain unaffected under any political circumstances. He is sure that it will transcend any changes or ruptures in the system, even the most radical ones, and in this sense, it will stay forever. During one discussion with his son-in-law, he mocks his naïve, almost childish attitude and calmly explains:

> …And the new people will rule? No, my boy, they took over the government from that asylum, not from us. Single people can be vanquished perhaps, but our structure is indestructible, millions of people work in our interest, without even realising it. You're a smart man after all, you even grasped the structure's nuclei, you just didn't understand what kind of structure it was. No one has fathomed us out yet. Not dumb writers with their naïve magic words 'bureaucracy' or 'nomenklatura' All that means nothing, they are chasing ghosts, but not us… I will be the first to throw a rock at that idiotic bureaucracy, we don't need people like that, all they are is ballast, their place can be occupied by anyone, by any kind of ballast… You can convene a hundred conferences or summits, you can declare that we don't exist any more, but we're still here, we're definitely still here.[3]

The narrator recalls his trip with his father-in-law's personal driver, Kaziukas, who represents a faithful servant to power. At a certain moment, Levas realizes that he began involuntarily identifying himself with the power of his father-in-law just by sitting next to Kaziukas and watching the activities of this dutiful butler:

> Once I drove with Kaziukas through all of Lithuania, He was driving me from Palanga, and at the same time performing his primary duty: collecting

tributes for Father-in-Law. I sat in a limousine with tinted windows, real leather seats, a radiotelephone and a Japanese television. I had been too long in the sun and was slightly light-headed, so everything seemed a tad unreal. I briefly felt like I was the real owner of the limousine, and looked contemptuously at the shitty little cars as we passed them one after another. For a first and only time, I felt like I was the centre of the world. That afternoon I ruled the world and viewed it disdainfully through my squinting eyes. I was ashamed. I'm even ashamed now that I remember it, but that's how it was.[4]

This passage contains an implication of how the seduction of power works. Even a person like Levas, while reluctant to give himself up to the role of performer like Kaziukas, is, nevertheless, seduced by the very possibility of being one of those who have real power over other human beings. This unusual sensation is one of the impulses to surrender to power in the hope that, one day, you will be the one who gives all the orders and exercises total control over individuals. The trip allows the narrator to grasp the hierarchy of power and experience how being seduced by the possibility of having power can affect any individual, even one who hardly aims at control over his fellow human beings.

Through the dialogues between Levas and his omnipotent father-in-law, Gavelis uncovers an ugly truth about the Lithuanian character and the limits of mutiny against the Soviet regime. In the same way as in *Vilnius Poker*, the writer conveys doubts about the final results of any movement directed against the regime. Levas' father-in-law remains steadfastly indifferent to the arguments that people calling for the disruption of the current regime will eventually be able to dismantle its mechanisms. He explains to Levas that people who are demonstrating against power are nothing but a crowd that hardly even needs to be scattered, as he is fully confident that it will take care of this by itself:

There's a crowd. Some of our people are frightened of that new movement, perhaps you heard – there was one that made itself known a week ago. The namby-pambies were scared. But I tell you, they're nothing. It's a crowd. They're Lithuanians after all. Did you ever see a mad dog chained up by his doghouse? He's angry, simply horrible, and it seems that if you unchained him – he would tear you to pieces then and there. But what happens when he breaks the chain? He runs around like a crazy, barks at the air and rolls around in the grass until you catch him and chain him again. And then… Most important is what happens next. Does he furiously start to bite the chain? Does he become mortally dangerous? No, my dear, he goes into his doghouse and falls asleep, tired and hungry. We will once again tie up the dog with a chain – and that's it. Let him run around, roll in the grass and catch air for the time being.[5]

These ideas disturb and derail the narrator. No matter how hard he argues with his father-in-law, the latter's cynical logic seems almost irrefutable. It is not only logic and experience that comes from the mouth of this Communist Party functionary, however; it is also the voice of power. It is a kind of power that is not afraid to withdraw or temporarily disappear from the eyes of the public. It is a form of power that is capable of coming back when it is least expected.

In the end, Gavelis offers neither an easy, upbeat ending nor an optimistic future. However, he does not claim that the future will necessarily go in one direction or another. Ultimately, he is not a futurist but a fiction writer who has created one more narrative of a possible world. Whether Levas' society finally succumbs to the ominous vision sketched by the father-in-law or whether it exits the twilight of postcolonialism depends to a large extent on the Lithuanians themselves. Although the metaphor of the dog let off the chain is not very flattering, there is a hint in it that should be taken seriously, especially in the current political climate and Russia's ongoing assault on one of its closest neighbors.

***

Though the English translation of *Memoirs of a Life Cut Short* was only made available almost twenty years after its original was first published in Lithuania and tells the story of a life related to a distant Soviet past, it remains a book that exhibits no signs of being outdated in any way. This short novel still deserves a close reading and remains full of potential to capture the mind of a serious reader looking for answers to his or her questions about the (vanishing) past. In addition to a profound inquiry into the essential features of the Soviet system even before it collapsed, it provides some more general insights into how power originates and how it seduces, corrupts, and finally enslaves young and aspiring individuals who might have served humanity better if they had been strong enough to resist this sweet temptation.

However, the novel is far less gloomy and less loaded with images of various forms of violence (including sexual abuse) than the 'nightmare' of *Vilnius Poker*, as its translator Elizabeth Novickas labeled it. In many ways, it is a remarkable fictional narrative that carries somewhat less 'weight' than *Vilnius Poker* but nonetheless demands a close reading into a system in which a human is destined either to disappear in his/her meager existence on the margins of the system (like Tomas, who is forced to give up his career as a highly promising scientist) or otherwise to act desperately and submit themselves fully to the service of the regime. If an individual gives up his/her ideals, they will be consumed by the power of the regime. This path is much riskier, as an individual who chooses to build his/her career in this way will eventually fall prey to monsters like Levas' father-in-law, who seem to be able to transcend any system and re-emerge as no less powerful and enduring figures in a postcolonial world.

Notes

[1] See, for example, Samalavičius. "Lithuanian Prose and Decolonisation," 409–428.
[2] Gavelis, *Memoirs of a Life Cut Short*, 74-75.
[3] Ibid, 196.
[4] Ibid, 132.
[5] Ibid, 198.

Works Cited

Gavelis, Ričardas. *Memoirs of a Life Cut Short*. Translated by Jayde Will. Glasgow: Vagabond Voices, 2018.
Samalavičius, Almantas. "Lithuanian Prose and Decolonisation: Rediscovery of the Body." In *Baltic Postcolonialism*, edited by Violeta Kelertas, 409–428. Amsterdam/New York: Rodopi, 2006.

CHAPTER IV

ORWELLIAN LESSONS:
THE ENCHANTED CITY
BY ROMUALDAS LANKAUSKAS

A year before Ričardas Gavelis published his *magnum opus*, *Vilnius Poker*, the same publishing house, Vaga, published Romualdas Lankauskas' novel *The Enchanted City*.

It was a curious period in late Soviet history. Though Mikhail Gorbachev's discourse on *glasnost* and *perestroika* circulated widely in the public sphere and was much talked about in the West as a sign of potentially fundamental and long-lasting reforms, this new course taken by Moscow was met with caution and incredulity by local authorities in most Soviet republics. Local Communist Party leaders were still convinced that the widely advertised course of change would soon be overturned and things would continue as usual. However, the discrepancies between the rhetoric coming from the Soviet central TV channel in Ostankino Tower and local media were becoming increasingly and uncomfortably visible. These thought-provoking differences were, of course, observed by many individuals hoping for even modest systemic shifts. Though the chances were high that Gorbachev's *perestroika* would meet the same fate as Khrushchev's Thaw a few decades previously, some intellectuals, writers, and editors saw it as an opportunity to take on previously forbidden or risky topics and expand the existing boundaries of freedom of speech. While the censorship authorities (known as Glavlit) continued their activities, they did so with less fervor than before.

Romualdas Lankauskas (1932–2020) – a well-known Lithuanian author of some twenty collections of short stories, novels, and several books for children – had previously tested the boundaries of the permissible, especially in his writings focused on the repatriation of inhabitants of the Klaipėda Region (previously known as Lithuania Minor) to Germany in 1958–1960. During this period, due to an agreement between West Germany and the Soviet Union, a number of people of German origin residing in Lithuania were allowed to move either to West Germany or to the DDR. Lankauskas was one of the very few Lithuanian writers who reflected on this dramatic and complicated process and its social and cultural consequences in his novels and short stories. There were also other issues where he attempted to cross the boundaries of the acceptable.

Moreover, his relationship with Soviet authorities was always complicated. Throughout the Soviet era, he was a notable and widely read fiction writer and an abstract painter – as such, he was a usual suspect. Additionally, he often tackled uncomfortable themes and topics not only in his fiction but also in critical essays published in Lithuania's leading cultural and literary periodicals. Unlike during the first post-war decades, however, censorship in Soviet Lithuania gradually changed during his time. Consequently, during the last two Soviet decades, established writers who expressed a certain criticism about the realities of the day were tolerated to a certain degree. The regime could no longer maintain the role it played after the war when any kind of dissent was crushed mercilessly and brutally.

A writer who was also one of the pioneers of post-war abstract art in Lithuania and well-known for his critical attitude toward the Soviet authorities, Lankauskas eventually became a *spiritus movens* and founder of the Lithuanian PEN Club, established in 1989 as the first national organization independent of Soviet supervision. He remained committed to the role of a public intellectual and continued to write opinion essays on Lithuanian politics and social life until the end of his life.

The Twilight Zone

Lankauskas' short novel *The Enchanted City* was another attempt at targeting previously forbidden themes. The novel, written in an Orwellian manner, provides a narrative about an individual who finds himself in a foreign city and realizes that strange circumstances have doomed him to remain in it, albeit for reasons that seem to be beyond any rational explanation.

The beginning of the novel does not seem to promise any unusual or dramatic events as the unnamed protagonist (eventually, the reader learns that his name is Bernardas Kunas – a middle-aged intellectual who has written an art history manuscript that will shortly be delivered to his publisher) unexpectedly decides to take a break during a long trip and gets off his train, intending to take some rest and get acquainted with a city he was previously unfamiliar with. However, despite his good intentions, the idea of leaving the train on which he was traveling proves to be a fatal decision, provoking unintended consequences.

After walking around the Old Quarter of the city he decides to visit, the narrator fails to find a way back to the railway station. The people he encounters on his way, as if by agreement, all refuse to point him in the right direction, and finally Bernardas realizes that he has missed his train. After being unable to show up at the railway station on time, he has no other option than to spend a night in a local hotel. Yet even this proves to be difficult as he learns that all the hotels in the city are fully booked. Luckily, though he left his luggage and belongings on the train, he finds out that he has his passport and some money. All these turn out to be prerequisites to booking a night's stay in a hotel.

At first, the protagonist does not seem to take his situation seriously. Despite the inconvenience of an interrupted trip, he only blames himself for his negligence and hopes to sort things out the next morning at the latest and board the next train. While talking with the hotel receptionist, however, Bernardas notes a photo of the railway station hanging on the wall.

> I looked again at the picture of the train station on the poster that hung behind her on the bluish wall. Why was I not there now? Why did the train leave without me? In fact, things went very badly. But who could I blame? Of course, only myself for that unforgivable carelessness, I went too far from the station, burned myself up by loitering and ended up wandering in a nondescript city. Well, be that as it may, why must I incessantly reproach myself: after all, could I have imagined before that none of the inhabitants of this city would show me the way to the station? It was really impossible to predict, such a thought did not even cross my mind. If only we knew what awaited us.[1]

Comforting himself with the thought that this unexpected situation would be solved no later than the following morning, Bernardas goes to sleep – only to be awakened by a telephone in the middle of the night. When he picks up the phone, an unknown voice directs him to check his desk drawer. After reluctantly following the order, he finds a message urging him to leave the city as soon as possible before it is too late.

Early in the morning, Bernardas checks out of his hotel and, with the help of the hotel's receptionist, manages to locate the railway station he was unable to reach the night before. However, when he reaches the station, the saleswoman refuses to sell him a ticket on the basis that he did not inform the authorities of his exit from the train or of his visit to the city. Instead, she redirects him to Grandiosas Generalpijus, the head of the railway station, who is the only person who can resolve this uncomfortable situation. Bernardas finds himself in a Kafkaesque situation when, during his meeting with Grandiosas Generalpijus, he is informed that he has violated the rules of the city and therefore has to fill in a mandatory questionnaire.

This task, however, turns out to be more complicated than he expected, as the secretary of the head of the railway station refuses to accept a questionnaire filled in by hand. She insists that he has to present a typed copy. As Bernardas does not know any copyist in the city, the secretary is kind enough to send him to a friend of hers who is in need of money and thus is taking on some extra jobs. Finally, the narrator receives a typed copy of the questionnaire he has previously filled out by hand, but even after fulfilling this requirement, he is not allowed to board the next train and leave the city. Taken aback by this absurd situation, Bernardas soon learns that there is a manager of the whole city who takes on different roles (including the head of the railway station), and it is he who has the sole power to make decisions that affect any person who is (or happens temporarily to be) under his jurisdiction.

The depiction of the city in the novel is rather abstract. Lankauskas avoids any direct allusions to Lithuanian urban centers of his time, and the characteristics of the unnamed city where the protagonist is destined to stay are too general to be associated with any particular Lithuanian locality. However, the location's abstractness and lack of peculiar features only strengthens the text's emotional and psychological impact. The city described by the writer could be any city in the territory of Soviet Lithuania or, in fact, in any other part of the Soviet Union because it can easily match Lankauskas' description: a beautiful but neglected Old Quarter, dull and gray new residential quarters (known as *mikrorayons* in the Soviet period), a generic statue of a political leader in the center of the city, etc. However, as the protagonist communicates with other characters he meets in this strange city without any language difficulties, this seems to suggest that it is within the borders of his native country.

The situation soon gets more difficult, as after being unable to board the train or buy another ticket, Bernardas is forced to stay another night in this strange city. To his dismay and horror, he realizes that he will not be admitted to the hotel as it is full. The other hotels in the city are full as well, and he faces the hard prospect of spending the night in the open air as the rain approaches. Luckily, Bernardas meets a kindred spirit – an unacknowledged yet gifted artist named Klaudijus who makes his living by painting the interiors of newly built or refurbished houses. This chance acquaintance provides a way out of a desperate situation: he offers Bernardas an informal assistant's job so that he can earn some income to pay for his meals and raise money to buy a ticket to escape the unfriendly city. This, however, also turns out to be more difficult than Bernardas imagined. Additionally, he learns that the only way out of the city is the railway. Some time ago, there had been an accident, after which the adjoining territories had been subjected to poisoning, and even while taking a train, one has to use a gasmask to avoid death or a possible illness. Thus, his plan to leave the city alone in a clandestine way is compromised.

Moreover, Bernardas is soon arrested and detained in a psychiatric hospital for his refusal to conform to the official regulations of the city and for insulting the city's leader, Grandiosas Generalpijus (who also happens to be the head of the railway station), where he is enforced to undergo treatment for a mental disorder. His doctors threaten him with lengthy confinement unless he agrees to take the prescribed medicine and give up his earlier convictions that they say led to his confinement. Though the description of how Bernardas is treated during his isolation in the psychiatric ward is rather abstract (the reader only learns that he does not take the prescribed pills and refuses to cooperate with the supervising doctor), the narrative contains inferences to the treatment of dissidents in Soviet psychiatric hospitals. This theme was thoroughly researched in 1977 by Sidney Bloch and Peter Reddaway, who recently subjected the topic to another historical overview.[2]

Though Lankauskas does not provide any detailed descriptions of the 'therapy' applied to the patients of this institution, some passages reveal the absurdity of the apparent methods. After spilling a prescribed pill and leaving his bed in his ward, Bernardas looks out from the window and contemplates the therapeutic procedures applied:

> In the courtyard, to the right of the window, Bernardas saw several poles painted in various colors, called healing poles: the sick had to try to climb them, and the one who, after long attempts and with great effort, reached the top was considered cured. He was soon discharged. Cabbage stalks were also extensively used for treatment, as it was believed that they had a positive effect on thinking, helping one to separate harmful ants from the rest. It was necessary to eat about a kilogram of them every day. When Bernardas once jokingly asked if this would eventually turn him into a rabbit, his portion (or dose) of the stalks was immediately increased.[3]

It is difficult to say whether, at the time of writing the novel, the author knew anything about the term 'punitive medicine' coined by Aleksander Podrabinek.[4] However, his ironic outlook seems to contain some essential and quite accurate knowledge about the absurd procedures applied to the patients of Soviet psychiatric hospitals, especially those doctors who 'treated' patients supposedly suffering from 'sluggish schizophrenia' (discovered by Russian psychiatrist Grunya Sukhareva and developed for several decades by notorious though internationally recognized Soviet psychiatrist Andrei Snezhnevsky) or any other illnesses diagnosed to them because of their uncompromising views about the communist regime. Though it is highly plausible that Lankauskas possessed some knowledge of how psychiatry was abused in the Soviet era as evidence was passed on by word of mouth as well as in *samizdat* publications, he confined the narrative of *The Enchanted City* to a few absurdities of this kind of treatment and avoided further digressions on the topic, which was still dangerous during the Gorbachev era. Nevertheless, the episodes of Bernardas' stay in the hospital are constructed so as to reveal not only the absurdity of the treatment but also the true motives behind the treatment program. During one of his several conversations with Doctor Fokas, who is in charge of his treatment, Bernardas learns that acknowledging his former attitudes and formally apologizing to the authority of Grandiosas Generalpijus is all it takes to get out of this grim and menacing institution. The protagonist, however, declines the doctor's intrusive suggestion to write a document publicly rejecting his previous views and acknowledging and expressing his loyalty to the unquestionable authority of Grandiosas Generalpijus.

Bureaucracy as Colonial Power

Like Gavelis, who never used terms like 'colonization' or its derivatives in his writings except when mentioning it in passing in his novel *Seven Ways to Commit Suicide*, Lankauskas avoids this category, most likely for the same reason. As mentioned earlier, the term 'colonialism' was largely expropriated by the ideological vocabulary of Soviet institutions that maintained that any form of colonialism was purely and solely a Western and capitalist enterprise. Power in *The Enchanted City* is mainly exposed through almost anonymous bureaucratic institutions managing the daily activities of the city's inhabitants. Quite often, these activities turn out to be devoid of any meaning or purpose, like, for example, the house refurbishments carried out by Klaudijus, who employs Bernardas as an assistant to save him from financial difficulties. In a conversation with Bernardas, Klaudijus reveals the futility of this commission as the building will be demolished as soon as the refurbishment works are over.

The novel is packed with equally absurd situations. One of them, as already mentioned, is related to the protagonist's involuntary stay in the city, which he intended to visit as a break on his trip to another place. Not being allowed to board his train again, Bernardas is forced to stay in an unnamed city until Grandiosas Generalpijus, the head of the railway station, approves another ticket for him. This turns out to be a more complex procedure than he initially expected. Thus, Bernardas faces the absurd situation of filling questionaries again and again, being forced to wait indefinitely until Grandiosas Generalpijus is in the right mood to sign his papers. However, this mood never comes.

Lankauskas constructs his main protagonist in a different manner to how Gavelis represents Vytautas Vargalys in *Vilnius Poker*. The protagonist of *The Enchanted City* is depicted not as a resistance fighter or a conspirator against the prevailing regime but as a more or less typical citizen. Bernardas Kunas is a professional art critic with no exceptional past or records of dissent or involvement in any activities against the regime. In this sense, he is very different from Vytautas in *Vilnius Poker*, whose biography is far more colorful (and complex), to say the least. Perhaps Lankauskas, who is well-known in the context of Lithuanian literature for the restraint of his narratives, consciously chose to depict a somewhat gray character devoid of any 'black holes' in his past but who, nevertheless, falls prey to the authoritarian system headed by Grandiosas Generalpijus.

Throughout the novel, Bernardas is presented as an ordinary individual living an ordinary life (the context of which is painted in very few strokes). It is striking that this individual appears to get into a very unusual situation of being forced to stay in an unfamiliar city without any aid or even sympathy from residents and the city administration. As the novel lacks any elaborate descriptions of individuals except those Bernardas encounters or who represent the structures of power, it is difficult to classify the characters. The antagonist, who personifies power, is presented very laconically. Lankauskas gives a succinct description of Grandiosas Generalpijus, who remains almost faceless and lacks any memorable personality traits. Like most bureaucrats, he acts so rigidly as to remain almost impersonal. The activities in which he is engaged during his office hours balance on the edge of absurdity. For example, after waiting patiently for hours to see the station master in a long queue with other visitors, Bernardas makes a desperate attempt to enter his office. To his great surprise, he learns that the bureaucrat is engaged in a game of dominos with an unnamed subordinate:

> The boss, with a plump, fleshy, very self-satisfied face, a massive square chin, inverted brown eyes (one was more set to the side), an extremely thick and short neck, and firm shoulders, sat leaning back in a wide chair at a desk furnished with different colored telephones, and next to him on a chair sat a thin, stooped man in a railwayman's uniform, holding a domino in his hand. At that moment, the big hairy hand of the boss was hanging in the air, but it suddenly came down with a thud and dropped a black oblong block marked with white dots on the table. The table shuddered with the impact. The boss triumphantly looked at the twisted man, completely crushed by the last, apparently decisive blow, stubbed out a cigarette in the ashtray (the smoke made it impossible to breathe), turned his head in my direction, narrowed

his eyes sharply and opened his lips in great surprise: How did you get in here?[5]

Except for a few abstract notes about Grandiosas Generalpijus performing the role of a station master, Lankasukas does not give any further details about this character. However, some of his official activities reveal the inherent absurdity of his public duties as well as his leisure activities:

> Controlling all the goods, bringing them by rail and sharing them with the city authorities, devouring the most delicious and healthiest food, and also pouring out the best drinks; he is the unstoppable champion of eating contests organized by high officials, and he can stuff seventy-three dumplings with garlic and pepper into his stomach, and drink ten liters of the best beer, and that beer, once passed through the kidneys, will later be able to be projected in a strong current to five meters, while the most capable men cannot overcome the four-meter ten-centimeter mark.[6]

Though this irony might well discredit the person, Lankauskas does not go too far with his irony or grotesqueness. The character of Grandiosas Generalpijus is further constructed through the lens of magical realism as, at times, he changes his bodily appearance, being capable of transforming himself into a dangerous wild animal, especially at night. This curious ability of a human person to be transformed into a kind of werewolf (or, more precisely, a wild boar) implies his extraordinary supernatural power.

Lankauskas' novel borders both realistic and conditional narration. The city described remains untitled; it is never related to any specific locality. The description of its urban character is also rather vague – the reader gets only a very general picture of the cityscape where the story takes place. In fact, it might be any city in the Soviet domain as they all became more or less homogeneous without any specific or distinctive features. The narrative takes regular shifts: a fairly realistic narrative is easily transformed by acquiring a mystical character and turns into a kind of fairy tale, as human characters (such as Grandiosas Generalpijus) acquire superhuman features and the individuals Bernardas encounters on the streets no longer resemble human beings. Instead, they remind him of ghosts or shallow holograms. The borderline between realism and hallucination is very fragile, and as the plot develops further, it acquires an almost non-realistic character, and the story slowly turns into a kind of dystopia. This gives Lankauskas' novel a distinctly postcolonial narrative, as crossing the borderline between realism and fantasy in David Punter's interpretation is a quality that is peculiar or even typical to postcolonial writing:

> The postcolonial [...] is a discourse of loss; what is also important to grasp
> is that, through the logic of hallucination, dream, the exotic, it is also a
> discourse of reversal, a reversal beyond the lucid and beyond the satiric, and
> that it is precisely here, rather than in any exorbitation of the political
> process, that its genuinely political power lies.[7]

Strangeness, unfamiliarity, and unrecognizability are the main themes of
Lankauskas' novel. On leaving the train, Bernardas hopes to walk around
the small and generally walkable city center; however, he eventually gets
lost while hurrying back to the station. None of the strangers he meets on
his way back is capable or even willing to point him in the right direction.
Even the people he encounters when trying to organize his enforced stay in
a foreign city act strangely and unnaturally. For example, the female
receptionist at the hotel turns him down because the place is fully booked;
however, she suggests he takes shelter in her aunt's flat. The next morning,
her human sympathy suddenly vanishes, and she sees him off with almost
undisguised hostility as if he had done something wrong. The secretary of
the railway station master exhibits some humanity by sending Bernardas to
her friend, who agrees to type up the questionnaire he has filled out by hand,
which is against the regulations (the typist, Lina, eventually becomes
Bernardas' love interest). Nevertheless, after he comes back to hand over
his questionnaire for the approval of the station master to be allowed to buy
a ticket and leave the city, she continues to act in a formal and bureaucratic
way. Throughout the novel, all the individuals Bernardas meets in this city
remain total strangers or ghost-like figures except for the painter Klaudijus,
whom he befriends, and Lina.

While Klaudijus and Lina are both presented as real and very humane
characters, the main antagonist, Grandiosas Generalpijus, remains utterly
strange and almost non-human. This strangeness is structured in part by the
latter's role as a mighty and impersonal bureaucrat – Grandiosas Generalpijus
embodies the highest political power in the city as he has the power to
permit ingress to and egress from a city surrounded by an infected, life-
threatening zone. Moreover, his character is created with a touch of magical
realism: he takes various forms in the life of the city, like being the main
speaker during a large meeting (the place is also the main area for public
gatherings and entertainment), where Grandiosas Generalpijus addresses a
large crowd of cheering (and submissive) city dwellers (except Bernardas,
who watches this public spectacle with undisguised scorn). Even Klaudijus,
who shares Bernardas' critical view of the city's administrator and
chameleonic leader, is afraid to show his position openly and discourages
Bernardas from showing his emotions because this might cause trouble for
both of them:

Klaudijus bent down and whispered in Bernardas' ear that he had laughed out of place and at the wrong time; it is said to be quite dangerous because it can be interpreted as an insolent outburst, disrespect for the words of the orator, and reported where necessary. And there is always someone capable of reporting: in this city, the citizens keep a close eye on each other, so no suspicious act goes unnoticed. When a deed and a light-hearted word, especially if it is critical of Grandiosas Generalpijus, is immediately heard and retold to him, often with lots of things being added in the retelling, a proper assessment is expected. Bernardas must keep that in mind.[8]

In another meeting that they are both required to take part if they want to keep their job, Bernardas learns that critics of Grandiosas Generalpijus are subjected not only to punishment but also to public condemnation. During the meeting under the circus cupola, the speaker conducting the public ceremony calls on everyone to publicly condemn a certain Teodoras Cimbolas, who is accused of challenging the authority of the city's highest manager. The master of the condemnation ceremony publicly announces:

> We are assembled here in this fine hall, which the wise fathers of our city have given us, together with the benefactor of us all, Grandiosas Generalpijus, a great lover and patron of the circus arts … to condemn the despicable pest Teodoras Cimbolas. (Pause. Surprise and commotion in the hall.) Yes, unanimously, without any reservations, we will condemn him as a malicious and deliberate slanderer who dared to speak disrespectfully about the bright personality of our beloved Grandiosas Generalpijus and all his fruitful activities (the angry lightning of the orator's eyes), when Teodoras Cimbolas tried to interfere and set the inhabitants of our cool, harmonious city against him, when… (sudden coughing, maybe he choked on saliva). But such a person has no place among us.[9]

Bernardas learns that this strange public gathering is a regular urban ritual. He even suspects that the person known as Teodoras Cimbolas never existed. He might be (and most probably is) just a fictitious character created by the city's management to warn the townspeople against criticizing the administration as there are grave consequences for engaging in such activities. Both the critic and the object of criticism remain a kind of phantom as neither of them appears on stage among the speakers.

However, at a certain point, Bernardas encounters a supernatural incarnation of Grandiosas Generalpijus, who appears in the dark as a wild boar, creating panic among the passersby. He learns that Grandiosas Generalpijus is especially fond of this particular appearance. Most often, he attacks women and takes great satisfaction in scaring them. It is also suggested (according to the city dwellers' gossip) that the city manager uses his power to make women become his concubines, especially when they aspire to be hired for jobs in his jurisdiction. Thus, his political power is inextricably linked with male power.

On the other hand, Lankauskas implies that power persists only because Grandiosas Generalpijus' subordinates (and the rest of society) take it for granted and never dare to question its legitimacy by continuing to submit to its most absurd requirements, refusing to think and act independently. Bearing in mind that the novel was written in a political context when Gorbachev's radical reforms of the Soviet system were being watched with trepidation in most Soviet republics, it is possible to understand why the author emphasized society's complete obedience and humility in fulfilling the authorities' most absurd demands. In 1988, there was almost no hope that the totalitarian and colonial system of the Soviet Union would soon collapse. Its power seemed completely unshakeable and almost eternal. The programmed 'eternity,' fortunately, was destined to last just two more – yet very long – years before its spectacular fall.

Lankauskas' novel demonstrates that he learned some lessons from George Orwell, especially *1984*. However, *The Enchanted City* is in no way a reproduction or adaptation of Orwell's ideas or his disturbing phantasmagoric vision of a possible future society. Lankauskas lived in a society that undoubtedly contained at least some of the essential features of the society of total control described in *1984*. He was also conscious of how far he could go if he wanted to publish his fictional images rather than assign them to a drawer, as there were not many more than two or three options from which to choose. Yet, in this sense, his strategy was different from Gavelis', who chose to write a narrative that went beyond the usual Aesopian language. Nevertheless, even if it was not meant for the drawers and had somewhat less resonance than *Vilnius Poker*, *The Enchanted City* eventually contributed to an understanding of the nature of an oppressive regime and the absurd mechanism of its bureaucracy, its forms of power and control, and its impact on individuals and the masses of the late Soviet period.

Notes

[1] Lankauskas, *Užkeiktas miestas*, 14.
[2] See Bloch and Reddaway, *Russia's Political Hospitals*; Bloch and Reddaway, *Soviet Psychiatric Abuse*.
[3] Lankauskas, *Užkeiktas miestas*, 47.
[4] Podrabinek, *Punitive Medicine*.
[5] Lankauskas, *Užkeiktas miestas*, 22.
[6] Ibid, 56.

[7] Punter, *Postcolonial Imaginings*, 108.
[8] Lankauskas, *Užkeiktas miestas*, 59.
[9] Ibid, 62.

Works Cited

Bloch, Sidney, and Peter Reddaway. *Russia's Political Hospitals: The Abuse of Psychiatry in the Soviet Union*. London: Victor Gollancz, 1977.
—. *Soviet Psychiatric Abuse: The Shadow Over World Psychiatry*. New York: Routledge, 2019.
Lankauskas, Romualdas. *Užkeiktas miestas*. Vilnius: Vaga, 1988.
Podrabinek, Alexander. *Punitive Medicine*. Ann Arbor, MI: Karoma Publishers, 1980.
Punter, David. *Postcolonial Imaginings: Fictions of a New World Order*. Edinburgh: Edinburgh University Press, 2000.

CHAPTER V

DECOLONIZATION:
THE POST-SOVIET NOVELS
OF RIČARDAS GAVELIS

Few literary scholars, if any, would argue today that *Vilnius Poker* did not pose the biggest challenge to Lithuanian literature during the late Soviet era. The novel was analyzed from various angles by numerous critics, and it became an object of analysis on university programs. However, Ričardas Gavelis' post-Soviet novels are often bypassed or even dismissed as lacking the quality of *Vilnius Poker* or some of his other novels and short-story collections written before the fall of the Soviet regime. Despite these persistent attempts, I have long refused to accept this view, though I agree about a certain mono-dimensionality of several of his later (post-Soviet) novels in comparison to his early work.

The most likely reasons his writing was bypassed in the post-Soviet period were his critical attitude toward post-communist socio-political transformations, his horror at seeing new avatars of the failed regime, and his contempt for the new class of politicians that originated in the emerging postcolonial society. Moreover, Gavelis never cared what the literary or political establishment thought of him, and he always distanced himself from official cultural or literary life. Looking at politics or official cultural policy with disdain and occasional contempt, Gavelis dissected the realities of postcolonial culture and politics in his novels, essays, and opinion columns published after the reestablishment of Lithuania's independence. Unsurprisingly, he was disliked by politicians, literary critics, and writers, with a few occasional exceptions.

However, realizing his role in the development of Lithuanian literature, he did not care about his reception among the critics or his peers. He was far more concerned about the reaction of readers in a postcolonial or post-communist culture, as readers often chose to give up reading books for more practical and financially rewarding activities. This was the social drama of the first post-Soviet decade when Lithuanian society faced the realities it had never encountered before while living in an iron cage. The situation of freedom was more than a challenge. It was an entirely different and novel world, and individuals born into and raised in the system of totalitarian dependence had to find a place for themselves. Often, it brought an end to illusions.

Money, Power, and Sex

Gavelis did not abandon his interest in the mystery of power, addressed in *Vilnius Poker* and *Memoirs of a Life Cut Short*, and he continued his inquiry into the issue after Lithuania's independence when it entered a post-communist phase. For example, *Prarastų godų kvartetas* (The Quartet of Lost Musings) is a passionate attempt to find out what urges individuals to strive for power. The author described the novel as 'anti-Gavelis-like,' most probably because its structure is less complex than that of *Vilnius Poker* or any other previous novel and, in certain respects, is reminiscent of the narrative of a fairy tale.

The plot is relatively simple, yet it is structured so as to capture, if not a typical, then a quite possible story of the early post-Soviet era. A nouveau riche businessman, Karlas Fergizas, returns to his home country from Russia with the intent to take over the state, hoping to subordinate it to his growing financial empire. His goals, however, clash with those of the self-made politician Gabrielius Taraila, a formerly ordinary individual who rose to unexpected heights during the Velvet Revolution. Thus money encounters political power, and this confrontation becomes an axis of the whole narrative.

Though the reader might initially be inclined to sympathize with Gabrielius, it soon becomes apparent that they are both aiming for total power and unlimited control over a society that finds itself in a transitory period. Gabrielius is described as a former tuner of musical instruments with a humble background who never dreamt of becoming a political leader until the national movement for freedom and independence created the possibility for individuals of his kind to move up the political ladder. The demolition of the previous regime created an opportunity for people like him to make an appeal to the masses and be elected to government.

Gavelis interprets this will for power through the medium of sexual desires. Gabrielius, described as an ordinary man with specific professional knowledge, is initially reluctant to realize what political power really entails. However, he discovers that his sexual desire is raised while addressing the crowd during the sort of mass rally that was so frequent before the collapse of the previous regime. He immediately feels immense sexual satisfaction he has never experienced in any other form. He realizes that his suddenly discovered ability to manage and manipulate crowds provides him with the utmost satisfaction, one that he was never even aware of before the night he delivered his speech to a cheering crowd. This newly discovered desire drives him to pursue politics and eventually catapults him into the ranks of the power elite. After experiencing an orgasm while entering the "vast vagina of the crowd," Gabrielius undergoes a complete transformation of his personality and acquires a new identity of a new-born political leader who pursues his desire to control and manipulate his compatriots:

> He stood alone at the foot of the cathedral bell tower, lonely as ever, yet all-seeing. The strange hand of the night gently caressed his face, showed him the way – not some path to find home, but the path of his whole life. He understood everything perfectly. He finally saw the sign. It wasn't just a profound vision – Gabrielius Taraila himself was reborn.
>
> People were amazed only by the instruments – some of them were very strange, sophisticated, or had never been heard of. But a real arranger, a real professional, could tune them as appropriate, turn them into the desired orchestra to tighten up the music that he needed. Gabrielius unconsciously thanked the gods: it was only thanks to them that his father chose the most magical, most significant profession for him. A real tuner can tune the whole world. The real adjuster is the messenger of the gods. A real tuner can match everyone as appropriate, and in this way, he survives everyone, lives the longest in the world. Right to the end of this world.[1]

The newly reborn Gabrielius directs his sexual energy to an anonymous, genderless object – a crowd, which is able to satisfy his most refined desires like no woman can. This new kind of pleasure – to manage and manipulate the crowd – exceeds anything he has ever experienced. His unexpectedly discovered passion for ruling motivates him and enables him to climb up the pyramid of power, removing all the obstacles in his way.

Gavelis interprets the mechanism of power and political manipulation in exclusively sexual terms. Sexual passion drives Gabrielius' desire and gives him enormous power to overcome any difficulties, to shake off real or imagined competitors. Political power is represented by nothing other than the phallus – a symbol and a tool of power, control, and total manipulation over the crowd. Nevertheless, Gabrielius soon learns, to his dismay, that even power does not last forever. After a short period of political upheaval when the crowd cannot resist his male powers, it starts to disintegrate; fewer and fewer people turn up for his mass rallies. Finally, the crowd is fragmented, atomized, and gradually disintegrates. Continuing to speak at every rally, Gabrielius feels disappointed and even betrayed. His sexual energy diminishes with the disintegration of the collective vagina of the crowd.

> For a couple of years now, since the night of miracles, Gabrielius has been philosophically observing how the menacing crowd of the Cathedral Square was turning into a despicable mess. Not a single one of them pulsated with a lively rhythm anymore; all of them were amorphous and soulless. There was not an iota of the maddened mind of the mob left in any such gathering of people: it had been hollowed out to nothing and had ceased to be the least bit enticing. The shards of the crowd could not ignite a common core; each shard acted separately: they repeated some incantation, were interested in some thing. The crowd remained non-threatening and completely harmless.[2]

After losing the secret sexual bond with the crowd that enabled him to have satisfaction and manipulate his fellow citizens, Gabrielius is deprived of his newly discovered means of sexual satisfaction. However, he turns his energy to the bureaucratic orchestration of the state. This shift also enables him to set his eyes on Kristina, a mysterious assistant of the businessman Karlas Fergizas, his arch-enemy, who gradually takes the place formerly occupied by the erotic crowd in his imagination. In the meantime, Karlas discovers a passion for Gabrielius' abandoned wife, yet the romance is interrupted by her unexpected (and somewhat mysterious) death in a traffic accident.

Finally, both competitors fighting for control of their society – Gabrielius and Karlas – perish. Each dies in his own way: the state's law enforcement agencies destroy the latter's powerful corporation, while a virus planted by Kristina ends Gabrielius' life. This outcome implies that any form of power in a transitory society eventually meets its limits when competition for control comes into play. Moreover, Gavelis seems to suggest that in a post-communist (postcolonial) society, no single individual, no matter how mighty they may be, can ever aspire to the absolute or eternal power represented by the image of Them in *Vilnius Poker*. The ultimate end of Gabrielius Taraila's ascent to political power and his arch-enemy's failed attempt to gain dominance and control with the help of his financial empire indicate that any kind of power ultimately turns out to be illusionary and ephemeral in a society that has no shape at all.

The Quartet of Lost Musings marks a turning point in Gavelis' work. Though the writer regularly looks backward and examines the origins of postcolonial society because it is primarily the colonial past that laid the foundations for its present (and quite ugly) shape, in this novel, he directs his attention to what is happening here and now. On the other hand, it contains more elements of popular literature than any of his previous books, except, perhaps, *The Last Generation of People on Earth,* despite the fact that Gavelis always liked mixing genres. Most likely, the writer realized the important ongoing shifts in the local and global literary landscape and took the increasing influence of (Hollywood) movies on Eastern European imagination into consideration. It should also be remembered that when Gavelis was writing *The Quartet of Lost Musings*, readers' interest in literary fiction, and in reading books more generally, had declined significantly. The novel demonstrates a certain disillusionment of the author with the society he observed and his declining faith in the power of literary fiction as a form of cultural critique.

On the other hand, it also coincides with the author's general frustration with the period of highly controversial social transition (documented in his opinion columns in Lithuanian media) marked by skyrocketing criminality, corruption in the ranks of government, increasing public apathy mixed with occasional social hysteria, and the growing distrust of writers and intellectuals who briefly rose to public consciousness during the Velvet Revolution yet soon fell into disfavor both with the government and the public. *The Quartet of Lost Musings* is a testament to failed hopes and timid illusions and an initiation to a different world than the one once imagined while taking brief snapshots of its being locked behind the Iron Curtain.

Unlike most of his fellow writers, Gavelis refused to demonstrate any loyalty to the confused and chaotic politics of the post-communist era on the pretext of accepting its mistakes or imperfections as inevitable or even natural in a society that had no experience of managing itself. He abhorred the desire of the newborn class of politicians and political elders to rule and control a timidly free society in what had until recently been a socialist crowd fed on myths and lies. Being a caustic intellectual *par excellence* and a person of high integrity who was firmly committed to the principles of freedom, in his reflections on the society in the making, Gavelis refused to accept lies for truths or half-truths.

Writer, Power and the Return of *Homo Lithuanicus*

Septyni savižudybės būdai (Seven Ways to Commit Suicide) is another gloomy and disturbing narrative that contains elements of a thriller but was described by the author as "one more dark novel" to add to his list.[3] Though it was generally accepted coldly or ignored by institutional literary critics (like most of his other novels written during the post-Soviet period), it marks quite an important stage in Gavelis' literary career. First and foremost, it is the only novel where he discusses the writer's fate in the dramatically shifting landscape of post-communist society in great detail and muses on the marginalization of literature as well as the faults of his fellow writers. In certain respects, it is a fictionalized commentary on a changing postcolonial society despite Gavelis boldly embracing some aspects of popular culture and exploring the possibilities of a literary thriller. The book might also be interpreted as a persistent and sharp social critique (typical of modern rather than postmodern literature), as Gavelis expresses his critical view on the ambiguous transformation of society. A harsh and insightful analyst of the Soviet Lithuanian culture and mentality that came into being during the long colonial period, he was no less critical of the emerging postcolonial society and individuals who were often no less disturbing than the characters of *Vilnius Poker*.

The main character of *Seven Ways to Commit Suicide* is Rimas Vizbara, a well-known writer in his early fifties who is aware of his aging and becomes more and more existentially disappointed and bored with himself, his society, as well as the rest of the (Western) world to which his country now belongs after escaping the Soviets' grip. His life is described as a slow suicide, and as Gavelis briefly explains in his postscript to the novel:

> Creative writing is usually neither great fun, nor a fun or profitable profession. Writing is only consistent and intentional suicide, and every true writer is an imaginary suicide. Life is conscious suffering, and the varieties of that suffering are best understood by suicidal creators. Writers try to recreate the world with words and sentences. Sometimes thoughts form from those words. Sometimes those thoughts teach, seduce, or kill the person reading them. Writers themselves are inevitably killed by their thoughts.[4]

Rimas continues to lead his ordinary life – writing novels, contributing essays and columns to popular media and some struggling literary weeklies and cultural monthlies, and participating in literary readings where he is surprised to meet young people and beautiful young women in the audience. He is both surprised and satisfied to find there are still a few individuals who read fiction and prefer to listen to writers' opinions while society at large is attracted to other things: money, career, influence, and power. He takes part in these habitual activities, however, with a certain detachment and touch of self-irony, as his readers seem to pose questions he is no longer interested in considering.

Moreover, Rimas' relationship with his wife has become ambiguous: when she left to conduct her business in Western Europe, their relationship gradually fell apart, though they continue to be officially married. His relationship with his father, a retired professor of mathematics, has never been easy, yet now it has become even more complicated. His father has become (or perhaps has always been) a cynic, yet he has maintained some distant affection for his son. There are some mysteries in his father's biography that Rimas tries to solve. For example, how did an academic mathematician of his kind manage to live a prosperous and otherwise worry-free life during the Soviet era? He is surprised that his father continues to act as a shadow adviser to the government even after he retires from his academic duties.

However, Rimas is engaged in writing, and writing turns out to be a destructive force that continues to kill him, albeit slowly:

> Rimas himself really felt the magical effect of literary suicide: even the remaining unpublished book of the destruction of the world sarkily darkened his life. First, he conjured up an unfortunate recurring dream in which he was a crumbling old man, futilely sniffing the smell of whiskey, paralyzed by festering hemorrhoids. Then that book broke up his family, kicking Nora out of the house and even out of Lithuania. Fearing that it would be blown up, the world began to fight back and bite back. Reality became fierce like a rabid dog and just as brainless. Standing under the shower jets at six in the morning, reality never took on any shape or meaning. Behind the shower curtain was only emptiness and meaninglessness – in that space, even viruses and Koch sticks were dead. And yet Rimas Vizbara still had to live.[5]

Rimas lives in a transitory society where values are changing rapidly. He realizes that the occupation to which he has devoted his life has lost its former significance since people are looking for things instead of answers to metaphysical problems or narratives about the meaning of human life. His close friend Juozas Verba (who turns out to have spied on him and reported him to the authorities under the previous regime) describes these changes even in more cynical terms. Juozas calmly explains to Rimas that in the new kind of society that began to take shape after the so-called Velvet Revolution, no one needs his books or his opinions as he has become a total loser in the game of life:

> "I read and comment on books that some people still need," said Juozas gloomily. "You write your own. So go on writing. Wrap yourself in your fantasies and get out of the way of real people in real life. Maybe you're a genius – I don't know. I don't read novels at all. But in life, you're a piece of shit."
>
> "A piece of shit?"
>
> "Absolute crap floating in a metaphysical hole. Maybe you have lots of money. Do you have assets? Or a determining influence in society? Maybe you can bribe some minister? Look at yourself, evaluate yourself realistically. Who are you?"[6]

Rimas initially refuses to agree with such drastic and undisguised cynicism. Publishers are still expecting his new novels, and the editors of dailies and weeklies look forward to his essays and articles. Although the ranks of the literary public have thinned, he is still invited to share his opinions with readers and even occasionally get in touch with pretty young women. However, after observing the emerging changes, he reluctantly agrees with Juozas' unpleasant and no less offensive diagnosis. The narrator notes:

> Rimas Vizbara spent years, even decades, exploring this world only to come to a startlingly banal conclusion. High IQ, amazing talent, and great principles are worth absolutely nothing in this city. Two things had meaning and value here: origin and acquaintances. In all cities of the world, parents and acquaintances determine a lot – but not absolutely everything. In this city, kinship determined everything. Everything else was irrelevant.[7]

Rimas finally experiences this himself. After meeting Greta, a gorgeous young model, he unexpectedly falls in love with her. Trying to impress his love interest, he takes her to a casino. He happens to know the casino's owner and occasionally spends time there. The night he arrives at the casino with Greta turns out to be an extremely successful one. He wins the jackpot – quite a substantial sum of money by the standards of the day.

However, his success turns into a total disaster. Shortly after, Rimas is attacked by a group of criminals. He finds himself chained to the wall of a cellar, where he is brutally tortured by a young nouveau riche man called Raima, who happens to be a drug dealer. As drugs have recently become fashionable, Raima supplies them to young people and manipulates them all, including Rimas' love interest, Greta. He gradually realizes that it was she who betrayed him to Raima and his gang.

In addition, he learns that it is not just for money that he has been abducted and chained in a basement somewhere. Raima seems to feel much more pleasure in having total control over imprisoning, maiming, and humiliating a well-known intellectual over whom he exercises his power. This feeling is above money, and although Rimas is told that he will hand over his casino winnings, he hardly expects to stay alive even after agreeing to give all his possessions to Raima. Eventually, a group of heavily armed men break into the basement and Rimas is saved by Poška – the owner of casino – and his small 'private army' since he has his own reasons to free him. Poška's philosophy states that no one abducts anyone from his property as he wants his clients to feel safe and protected. After all, it is his clients who generate income for his prosperous business.

Curiously, there is hardly a single reference to law enforcement in the novel, even though it is, for the most part, a crime thriller. Individuals, groups, and businesses (including those of a criminal nature) resolve their disagreements among themselves. This might be because Gavelis viewed state power structures with a certain distrust. His early novels are full of the metaphysical horror arising from the principles and methods applied by totalitarian power. His later prose writings reveal an equally cautious approach to the new mechanisms of post-communist (postcolonial) state power: the system is no less corrupt than the previous one and is often run by the same individuals (or their heirs), albeit now acting under the guise of the agencies of a liberal democracy.

As a committed libertarian, Gavelis was openly skeptical about the possibilities of the state in many areas of public life. The end of *Seven Ways to Commit Suicide* implies that there are other ways to solve problems, even when criminals are involved. One should not forget that the novel was written during the first post-Soviet decade when lawlessness and the criminal behavior of many actors, including state institution officials, was a reality; in fact, criminal organizations often had more power than the state. Gavelis was undoubtedly always on the side of the individual, not the state; however, his view of postcolonial individuals was no less complex or critical than his view of an amorphous transitory society.

It is not a coincidence that in *Seven Ways to Commit Suicide*, Gavelis returns to the issue of *homo lithuanicus*, which he analyzed in great detail in *Vilnius Poker*. He completes the portrait of this strange creature, adding new details to it. The novel's narrator concludes that *homo sovieticus* and *homo lithuanicus* were two sub-species of ant-people that existed during the previous regime. However, after the fall of the Soviet Union, they mated and produced offspring, making their classification, if not impossible, then at least extremely difficult:

> The empire of ants and the Iron Curtain fell, and *homo sovieticus* was wasted in its purest form in a terrible spasm. Now the avenue was ruled by the *homo neolithuanicus*: ants, dressed very smartly, carefully hiding their extra limbs. The people of postcolonial Lithuania seemed to have to be liberated, they had to turn into unseen mighty men of spirit, real Lithuanian giants, and they only became even more ant-like. They have not the faintest remnants of the spirit of pretense that *homo lithuanicus* possessed. Something was wrong here, but Rimas could not decipher the essence of that Lithuanian defeat.[8]

Even though he was an insightful writer, Rimas proved to be completely naïve in not being able to understand what the mutation of *homo lithuanicus* would end up being. He maintained the naïve hope that after escaping from the colonial yoke, his compatriots would be thirsty for freedom and the opportunities it provided. This did not happen. Rimas has a heated argument over this issue with his father, who calmed down his son's enthusiasm, claiming that Lithuanians "don't give a shit" about freedom – they only need shepherds, i.e., they want to be governed and are ready to please the authorities.

After initially arguing fiercely with his father, Rimas finally realizes that his cynicism is well-grounded, especially after he goes to the USA with a few fellow writers whose thinking and behavior correspond to the standards of *homo neo-lithuanicus*. This experience enables him to conclude that Lithuanian writers most likely belong to the *homo neo-lithuanicus* species. Rimas recalls the late Soviet era – an era of scarcity – when the authorities would deliver so-called 'Brezhnev packages' to 'worthy' citizens before the state holidays. Such food packages usually contained a frozen chicken, conserved peas, mayonnaise, and instant coffee. He remembers how people reacted to these goods and likens their reaction to the release of serotonin in the brain, making them experience a "small orgasm."

Rimas immediately recognizes the same gaze when he and two fellow writers are invited by an émigré Lithuanian to visit his Manhattan apartment during their trip to the US. At one point, the host generously opens his wardrobe full of new and used clothes and generously urges them to pack anything they like and take it back home. He immediately recognizes the emotional pattern when the other writers experience the same orgasm upon being offered these luxury items for free. After the host asks if their eyes flicker at the sight of such an abundance, the narrator calmly observes:

> No, they didn't flicker – their eyes were glassy as if after a dose of drugs. The usual Lithuanian cultural stench became much stronger; those poor people's hands began to tremble, they simply didn't know what to do anymore. Rimas thought both writers were about to pass out. Like those people of the communist universe while opening the parcels delivered to them during the hunger years. Those ant-people haven't changed a bit in ten or more years, not even being affected by the random change of eras. Not even the crazy smells and sounds of New York hardened their ways.[9]

Rimas concludes that his colleagues going wild at the sight of free commodities were hardly people in need. Yet they represented the same type of mentality of Soviet Lithuanians who went mad at the sight of the Brezhnev packages. He realizes that even intellectuals did not get rid of their habits of thinking and acting. Instead of reporting on their colleagues for the housing provided by the authorities as they did during the Soviet years, they were now grappling with each other, fighting for awards, scholarships, and other bonuses distributed by the state. Thus, neither *homo sovieticus* nor *homo lithuanicus* died out like the dinosaurs or other prehistoric animals but continued their existence as a no less ugly and pathetic creature Gavelis labels *homo neo-lithuanicus*. Both Gavelis and the novel's protagonist Rimas seem to agree that this resistant subspecies does not succumb to eradication – at least, not in the near and foreseeable future.

Looking back on Gavelis' observations after a quarter of a century, one can only marvel at the author's insight. Lithuanian writers and other intellectuals – with only a few exceptions – remain in the captivity of this persistent matrix. They often give up their opinions and refrain from criticizing the authorities, reciting banalities and safe rhetoric in exchange for prizes and other financial rewards. Consequently, it is not surprising that they become less and less significant, being looked upon as no more than service providers.

The Last Novel

Ričardas Gavelis' last novel, *Sun-Tzu's Life in the Holy City of Vilnius*,[10] translated by Elizabeth Novickas and published by Pica Pica Press, is, like most of his previous titles, neither an easy nor an entertaining read. Originally published in Lithuanian in 2002, it is a chilling, often gloomy, somewhat desperate piece of literature and, at times, even more depressing than his several previous works in this genre. Having written a sequence of several 'noir' novels (as he called them himself) that were full of unsolved mystery and violence and often contained a large repertoire of threatening, shocking, and even repulsive images, the writer continued his cold-blooded and merciless exploration of the dark side of the human soul as well as his inquiry into a society created and eventually perverted by humans themselves until his untimely death.

To those already familiar with at least a few of Gavelis' titles preceding *Sun-Tzu's Life*, his last novel would hardly come as a surprise. Yet, at the same time, reading it requires some conscious inner strength to enter the dark, cynical, and bizarre underworld of what came into being after the collapse of communism – a process he depicted so vividly, masterfully, and no less mercilessly. Any perceptive reader of Gavelis' poignant prose would most possibly agree that he was, as the afterword to the English translation explicitly states, "a master of the macabre." However, despite seemingly being a cold and somewhat overly rational writer providing a "surgical" view of an irreversibly perverted society, he nevertheless had at least a small amount of optimism. The final chapter of his last novel contains this tiny hint of hope as he concludes his narrative with a few lines about a handful of strangers who, unbeknownst to themselves, keep the world going.

After providing a thrilling narrative about the fall of the almost totally corrupt and degenerate city of Vilnius that he also chose to destroy in one of his earlier novels (*The Last Generation of People on Earth*, 1995), Gavelis starts the final chapter, titled 'The Righteous Ones,' of his last novel with a hopeful narrative about its possible redemption:

> Thirty-six righteous souls live and have always lived on the earth, and their purpose is to justify the world in God's eyes. The righteous ones do not know each other, and in life they get by poorly. If someone finds out they are one of the thirty-six righteous souls, they instantly die a painful death, and their place is taken by another somewhere in an entirely different corner of the world. These righteous souls uphold people's existence in the world. If they didn't exist, God would have destroyed the human family a long time ago.[11]

Though Gavelis speaks about the world and a human family in this brief concluding section of the novel, it is reduced to the one and only 'eternal' city he knew so well – Vilnius, where almost all the plots of his early and later novels were set. His relationship with this city was always ambiguous – he seems to have loved and hated it at the same time, as can be explicitly seen in its depiction in his *magnum opus*, *Vilnius Poker*, which was also the first book of the so-called Vilnius trilogy (made up of *Vilnius Poker*, *Vilnius Jazz*, and *The Last Generation of People on Earth*). As Gavelis once remarked in his conversation with literary critic Alijušas Grėbliūnas, "I mystify, glorify, and imprecate this city, but first and foremost, I love it."

Nevertheless, as any sensitive reader will observe, he most often depicted Vilnius as perverted, toxic, and, probably, the most dangerous place on earth where anything could happen to anyone – or had already happened. The urban milieu described in *Sun-Tzu's Life in the Holy City of Vilnius* is no exception. Whatever this city happens to be, it is far from a holy place, even if it contains more houses of worship and a variety of other religious structures than any other Lithuanian city. One could argue that the "holy city of Vilnius," as described in Gavelis' last novel, is far closer to the biblical Sodom and Gomorrah than any sacred site as the novel's title deceptively (and consciously) implies. Nonetheless, the writer was no cynic; rather, it can be concluded that Gavelis finally chose to transgress the macabre scenography of his last novel to bring a tiny beam of light to his world of ultimate darkness.

Sun-Tzu's Life once again focused on the city that, with only a few exceptions (e.g., *Memoirs of a Life Cut Short*), he made the continuous subject and center of his prose writing throughout his literary career. In many aspects, this novel is a continuation (but not a repetition) of his usual themes, the most important of them being power and various forms of domination and subjugation. Before writing this novel, which ultimately turned out to be his last one, Gavelis had already explored many aspects of it in his preceding novels centered on the issue of power. Some might even call it a life-long obsession. But was it really an obsession?

Questions like this are probably futile. A writer decides why he or she pursues this or that subject himself or herself. Gavelis chose to struggle with the enigma of power as he most probably felt it was vital, especially in certain social conditions. It was undoubtedly essential in the era of Soviet domination, but it also turned out to be no less important after the collapse of that oppressive regime, as the newly emerging politicians and political gangs were no less thirsty for power than their predecessors. Gavelis took politics seriously, but he had no taste for politicians. As he remarked in one of our conversations a quarter of a century ago, he could only "detest the caste of politicians."[12]

Gavelis turned out to be both an eye-witness and a bold interpreter of post-communist transformations while describing the paradoxical realities of a society undergoing a painful, ambiguous, and often confusing social change. He did not buy the idea that a regime change (no matter how radical it is) can automatically bring out a perfect society. Far from it. Being a writer of high moral integrity who was so critical of the Soviet regime, and generally all totalitarian regimes, in *Vilnius Poker*, Gavelis had no illusions about the post-communist developments. His evaluations were cold, reserved, and occasionally cynical. He never believed that society could soon eliminate a burden of history that large. His literary reflections on post-Soviet society were thus far from flattering. In fact, each of his novels written after the fall of the Soviet regime was gloomier than the last, as if he had lost hope in the redemption of post-communist society.

In his last novel, *Sun-Tzu's Life in the Holy City of Vilnius*, Gavelis narrates the tale of his protagonist, who is born into a family of a dissenting scientist and follows his mission of deconstructing the world. Secretly working in his own private laboratory in his apartment, the protagonist's father hopes to create a better world. However, he ultimately fails dramatically: one day, he is found with his head cut off. The author makes no secret of the fact that the scientist was murdered by the very system he had secretly tried to investigate. The victim's son is only invited to witness the death and sign the papers.

Eventually, the protagonist, who tries desperately to understand what happened to his father, discloses the official secret:

> Everything was more or less cleared up for me much later, rummaging through KGB archives and repeatedly questioning old security agents. At the time, all I understood was that my first father's head had been cut off. It

was an excessive punishment, one that no human deserves – even those living in Vilnius. I didn't deserve my punishment either: for what fault did the gods allot me precisely that kind of father and precisely that kind of mother? That's a rhetorical question the gods haven't answered to this day, not even in my dreams. On the whole, they don't answer any questions. You must give them and answer them all by yourself.[13]

Like most of Gavelis' novels, *Sun-Tzu's Life* has no real heroes. Even those characters who, like the protagonist's father, might be regarded as dissidents and fighters against the totalitarian regime turn out to be far more complex people and are actually non-heroic or even anti-heroic. The protagonist's father continues to stay with his wife even after discovering she has constantly been unfaithful to him, and this fact hurts his son, who cannot understand how such an attitude conforms with his father's ideals. On the other hand, his work to deconstruct the world he hates is equally ambiguous, for he hardly offers any alternative to the system he aims to deconstruct.

The protagonist, who bears witness to the social change and finally decides to take part in it, urged on by his mother, Gorgeous Rožė, is also devoid of heroic features. The author follows his moral regression, which becomes more and more obvious with time. As soon as he enters politics, he turns out to be a character who adheres to no moral code. He becomes an even more complicated individual who breaks almost all ties with his milieu, gives up his family ties, and considers himself to embody both good and evil, imagining himself above both as Friedrich Nietzsche's Superman: "I'm a man without a single face. All the more, a man without a single real name. You could call me the Archangel Gabriel. But you could call me Abaddon, too, even if I don't destroy the world with my gaze."

Eventually, the protagonist of *Sun-Tzu's Life* becomes disillusioned with politics and political action. This is how he turns into a cold and cynical ancient warrior who aims to destroy the humans that he considers to embody evil. At the same time, he becomes a perverted killer who not only destroys his enemies but also gathers a collection of their bodies in a secret Vilnius underground. This semi-conscious transformation is described in the following way:

I am called Sun-Tzu, I am a military leader, and my field of battle is the entire world, artificially compressed into the holy city of Vilnius. In addition, I am a collector: I collect and spiritually burn the cockles of the world, all the miscreants and scoundrels – all that is left of them is wailing and gnashing of teeth. My collection of surgical instruments is no worse than Albinas Afrika's collection of drums and drumlets. My only friend and supporter Apples Petriukas agrees with my way, even though he's not prepared to battle with anyone – he only attempts to understand God's eyes.

He says this is how he begins the twenty-first century; while I begin the twenty-first century in my own way.[14]

Taking shelter in the guts of the 'holy city,' the protagonist, now Sun-Tzu, goes on to dissect the bodies of his victims, occasionally aided by another character familiar from *Vilnius Poker* – the medical doctor and coroner Kovarskis, whom he invites to share his secret passion while still running the government. Curiously, the Kovarskis of *Sun-Tzu's Life* bears little resemblance to the old, exhausted doctor who discovers a special kind of illness called 'Vilnius Syndrome' in *Vilnius Poker*. Here, he is depicted as a crazy American-based expatriate surgeon sharing a certain kinship with the infamous Dr. "Death" Kevorkian, consumed by the passion of dissecting deceased people – an alter-ego of Vilnius' Sun-Tzu, who is likewise desperate, mad, and a cold-blooded destroyer of all forms of evil. The novel's protagonist seems to believe that a crazy perverted world deserves only equally crazy and perverted actions.

Reading Gavelis' last novel leaves one faced with a strange sense of guilt, or perhaps of shame, of dealing with a deeply disturbing or even perverted society made up of perverted people. However, by acknowledging and accepting this feeling, one might find a way out of the confusion. As the literary scholar and aesthetician James S. Hans thoughtfully remarked,

> The human need for victims in the face of the arbitrariness and relative unpleasantness of life is inexhaustible, it would seem, and readily finds an outlet in the expression of violence toward another animal, be the victim a human or some other species. This is precisely why it is so necessary to face shame at the center of human consciousness, for only that confrontation holds any hope of allowing us to escape from the endless symbolic shuffle of victims we search for every time we feel some resentment toward life and wish to get back at it.[15]

Be that as it may, Gavelis' last novel provides much food for thought, not only for those living in and experiencing a never-ending social transformation but also for those readers who encounter other forms of social or political madness in their immediate surroundings.

A close reading of *Sun-Tzu's Life* obscures how Gavelis moved far beyond the classical dichotomies peculiar to early postcolonial theory, i.e., those between the center and periphery, the colonizer and the colonized. His novel, set in the post-Soviet context, is more complex in terms of power relations, especially as the old power structures seem to have collapsed. However, the essence that made these relations possible has been maintained. As Deborah L. Madsen insightfully observed, "The colonial relationship, mediated through discourse, is not then a simple opposition between the colonizer and the colonized but a complex network of discursive, power, relationships."[16]

Notes

[1] Gavelis, *Keturių godų kvartetas*, 24.
[2] Ibid, 85.
[3] When I met Ričardas by chance in 1999, walking home with a few copies of his newly published book under his arm, he described the book he had written to me as "one dark black novel."
[4] Gavelis, *Septyni savižudybės būdai.*
[5] Ibid, 62–63.
[6] Ibid, 113.
[7] Ibid, 106–107.
[8] Ibid, 91.
[9] Ibid, 195–196.
[10] Gavelis, *Sun-Tzu's Life.*
[11] Ibid, 271.
[11] Ibid.
[12] Samalavičius, "A Conversation with Ričardas Gavelis," 52.
[13] Gavelis, *Sun-Tzu's Life*, 64.
[14] Ibid, 232.
[15] Hans, *Origins of the Gods*, 105.
[16] Madsen, "Beyond the Commonwealth," 8.

Works Cited

Gavelis, Ričardas. *Keturių godų kvartetas*. Vilnius: Tyto alba, 1997.
—. *Septyni savižudybės būdai.* Vilnius: Tyto alba, 1999.
—. *Sun-Tzu's Life in the Holy City of Vilnius.* Flossmoor, IL: Pica Pica Press, 2019.
Hans, James. *The Origins of the Gods*. New York: SUNY Press, 1991.
Madsen, Deborah L. "Beyond the Commonwealth: Post-Colonialism in American Literature." In *Post-Colonial Literatures: Expanding the Canon*, edited by Deborah L. Madsen, 1–13. London: Pluto Press, 1999.
Samalavičius, Almantas. "A Conversation with Ričardas Gavelis." *Lituanus* 65, no. 1 (2019).

CHAPTER VI

REVISITING COLONIAL HISTORY: NARRATIVES OF HERKUS KUNČIUS

Herkus Kunčius (b. 1964) is one of the very few Lithuanian writers who have made recent history the topic of their narratives and conceptualized crucial periods of the country's turbulent past. In many ways, his prose writing differs from any other Lithuanian author as, among many other things, unlike his peers, he did not study literature at university but got a degree in art criticism.

He approaches existential themes with utmost grotesqueness, irony, satire, and, most often, black humor, passionately unlocking and deconstructing realities of the past that were both shocking and absurd. His writing is hardly comparable to that of Ričardas Gavelis because Kunčius is a far less rationalist author; his novels are less eerie, depressing, and pessimistic than those of his famous predecessor. They are, however, full of biting, stinging irony and black humor. Next to intellectually subtle jokes, Kunčius does not shy away from much coarser humor, balancing on the border of profanity. There is often a rather deceptive thought that such a literary fabric is a little too light, shallow, or even superficial. Some literary critics recognize his unparalleled ability to create comic texts but do not want to interpret him as full-fledged fiction.

Since his debut novel titled *And the Bottom Will Always Hold* was published in 1996, Kunčius has produced a large number of books, primarily novels (*Past Frequent Tense*, 1998; *Ornament*, 2002; *No Mercy for Dushansky*, 2006; *A Lithuanian in Vilnius*, 2011; *Derwish from Kaunas*, 2014; *Stalin's Iron Glove*, 2019; and many others), as well as occasional collections of short stories (*To Betray, Disown, Slander*, 2007; *Tales of an Imaginary Country*, 2015), essay collections (*Full Moon Fun*, 1999; *Three Beloved Ones*, 2014), and plays for the theatre (some of them are collected in *Illuminated*, 2020). He might be considered one of the most prolific writers in present-day Lithuania.

The Intersection of Past and Present

Kunčius' novel *The Drunkard's Reader* (2009) can be read in different ways: as a witty, funny collection of narratives with no other goal than to amuse the reading audience or as an ironic and somewhat anthropological story about drunken customs in Soviet and post-Soviet Lithuania – a conscious revision of Lithuania's colonial past. In the latter case, there is certainly another layer beyond humor. The consumption of alcohol in the Soviet Union meant quite a number of things, beyond which it also performed certain ideological functions. Realizing that a sober consciousness is the state when one seeks answers to the most essential existential questions concerning the nation and the individual, excessive drinking was not only tolerated by authorities and management but even encouraged on various levels to persuade and eventually force the people of the colonized society to live and play the roles imposed on them without thinking about or criticizing the colonial institutions.

There is a short chapter in *The Drunkard's Reader*, the structure of which resembles a short story, named *Nashe kino* (Our Cinema) in Russian. Its stylistics are quite different from other parts of the novel, which are laid out according to the mosaic principle. The narrative – in which an elderly couple is getting ready for a night's sleep – connecting the Soviet era with the present takes place in the present day. After the man's wife falls asleep, he is restless, tossing and turning in bed, haunted by sad memories. From a few sentences, we learn that the old man is a descendant of a noble family who once had the title of a count.

In his memories, the beautiful life of an aristocrat is interrupted by the violence of the poor who ravage the estate, then episodes of the post-war Soviet era pass before his eyes like a movie. Count **Genams**, his mind swarmed by memories, shuts himself in the bathroom, where he performs a secret ritual every night: he examines relics that remind him of times gone by. Among these are the neatly folded uniform of a KGB colonel and a weapon stored in a pocket of his breeches:

> Soon, standing upright in his pajamas, the count is putting on tight breeches, wrapping up his shawl, and pulling on his boots.
> A uniformed officer looks at the count from the mirror.
> Angry, furious. With a mothballed suit jacket.[1]

In this chapter, which is only a few pages long, there are no big or significant events: the old man, succumbing to the flow of memories, briefly moves to the past. The officer's uniform and weapon, specially stored in the bathroom, help to bring back his memories. The author provides no more details about the deeds committed by the retired KGB colonel; however, the reader can easily imagine that his past contains a number of dark secrets. The character is not haunted by the demons of the past that haunted the protagonist of Ričardas Gavelis' short story *A Report on Ghosts*, in which the former KGB interrogator Jeronimas Šukys sees phantoms visiting his bedroom almost every night and, because of this, writes a report to the authorities.

The characters of Gavelis and Kunčius are in some ways connected and, in others, quite different. The main character of *A Report on Ghosts* is a retired interrogator who brutally maimed his victims in his youth. He willingly gives details of interrogations he carried out during his career in his report and maintains that he is absolutely innocent: he always acted in the right way, and it is the victims who are to be blamed. The character created by Kunčius is more mysterious – the reader learns nothing about his past activities, but the ritual he continues to perform every night is telling in itself. The old man feels better and more secure when he opens the box and puts on his old uniform. In this way, the past stays in the present, and there are no cracks in his biography. The ritual gives him back the old self he has to hide while living in the society that came into being after the collapse of the former regime that he seems to have served faithfully.

In one of his latest novels, *A Lithuanian in Vilnius*, Kunčius examines the problems of hybridity, identity, and personal integrity – characteristic of postcolonial literature. The action takes place in the present. When Vilnius is granted the status of European Capital of Culture, the novel's main character, Napoleonas Šeputis, takes the chance to visit his country's capital city. After getting ready to visit the European Capital of Culture, Napoleonas finds himself in an environment where grotesque characters have got rid of their old Soviet identity and put on new masks. For example, a teacher called Terese, a member of the national dance and song collective "with bright eyes and a shrill voice," who is traveling with Napoleon to the capital by bus, is full of extreme right-wing views. There are also customs officers who have lost their posts, cursing the whole world, and many other slippery characters. As the story progresses, the following characterization of the post-Soviet era is presented:

> In the land of Mary,[2] everyone has been lying to their heart's content for years: the government, radio and television, commentators, switchboards, even cult services. There was a competition to see who could lie most brazenly, cheat most disgustingly. Politicians and cobblers, ministers and statisticians, lobbyists and journalists, beauticians and political scientists, gamblers, laundresses and their employers lied.

Incited by curators, hypnotized by self-proclaimed managers, instructed by insolent producers, the "voice of reason," instrumentalists, artists, and other entertainers who were guessing everywhere, who were the most respected people of Lithuania just yesterday, began to lie.

That was the norm of the time. No one was surprised. Drenched with happiness, the folk sang and danced uncontrollably because they wished it would always be like this.[3]

Unlike Gavelis, who openly and mercilessly dissected *homo lithuanicus* in *Vilnius Poker* with the passion and insight of a sociologist, Kunčius, as a rule, avoids any theoretical or sociological interludes in fictional literary texts. Instead, he relies on literary imagery, the flow of occasionally absurd narrative, comic and ironic intonations, and occasionally openly grotesque and exaggerated language. However, in the fiction he constructs (which both describes the present and is full of retrospective excursions to Soviet society), an unexpectedly serious, somewhat sociological narrative emerges, highlighting some interesting aspects of a not-so-distant reality that have often not been reflected upon before. For example, in Gavelis' novel, some features of the Lithuanian "national culture" of Leonid Brezhnev's era are ironically discussed by the narrator:

In those dark times of persecution, the Lithuanian intelligentsia found great meaning in this house "at grandma's place." At the "point" of the main street, you could meet a Lenin Prize laureate and a monk, a professional pensioner and a dissident, an acclaimed poet and a hero of socialist work.

In this palace, from dawn to dusk, was liberty, equality, fraternity. The door was open to everyone. If the last drinker in the ale house, which would suddenly slam shut, had nowhere to go after midnight, he was let in and seated at the table. He would be filled up, given a snack. His worries were understood, he was surrounded with love.[4]

Here, Kunčius is referring to unofficial (night-time) places for the consumption of alcohol that existed outside the Soviet institutions but played their part in the culture and everyday life of the Soviet period. What he attempts to emphasize is a kind of 'democracy' that existed outside the official culture of bars and restaurants. Even when applying irony and grotesque, Kunčius provides some personal and valuable anthropological reflections on a highly ambiguous Soviet way of life.

In *A Lithuanian in Vilnius*, Kunčius uses the character of Napoleonas Šeputis – who embodies a complex set of eclectic post-Soviet features – to open up two planes of time: the Soviet era and the present, which has preserved elements of the former, albeit while putting them into another, even more curious puzzle. The main character initially resembles a good-hearted provincial chap but later becomes a kind of medium. At first glance, this combines distant eras, but at the same time, it deconstructs the adaptation strategies typical of the Soviet period, which, as the novel develops, not only have continuity but also provide considerable benefits. Some of the novel's memorable characters – for example, the director of the Cigar House – turn out to be employees of well-known colonial structures who, after the social transformation, began to work for new masters who represent the new security (intelligence) structures of the former empire continuing their regular activities in a postcolonial world.

In an article that modestly accelerated the arrival of postcolonial studies in the Baltic, Violeta Kelertas describes the situation of prose writing during the first decade of independence as follows:

> From the point of view of revival, modern literature in Lithuania, apparently oversaturated with dictates in Soviet times, now avoids reflecting reality. The result: huge gaps are left; the experience of liberation from the Soviet yoke and life under the conditions of a market economy are almost indescribable. All this is actually left to newspapers. Self-expression occurs in the comment section, where everyone who can access a computer 'reflects,' if not the situation, then, let's say, their colorful but poor Russified Lithuanian.[5]

In a number of novels, including *The Drunkard's Reader* and *A Lithuanian in Vilnius*, Kunčius creates a variety of situations and images that emphasize a certain continuity of habits of thought and action even after the previous regime and its networks of dependence have collapsed. He seems to imply that individuals and their consciousness are strongly affected by their previous experiences. Thus, even though the surface decoration and symbols change, many individuals continue to exist and act as if they still live in the pre-independence era. Kunčius' characters master the new language of a different society and learn their new roles quickly, but in their essence, they remain deeply committed to their former selves. However, unlike Gavelis, who explores this painful shift as a kind of tragedy, Kunčius makes it look like a colorful theatrical performance. However, despite choosing a different set of literary devices, he continuously observes the past in the present. Thus, his writings seem to conform with an observation made by John McLeod, who claims that

> 'postcolonialism' is not the same as 'after colonialism,' as if colonial values are no longer to be reckoned with. It does not define a radically new historical era. Nor does it herald a brave new world where all the ills of the colonial past have been cured. Rather, 'postcolonialism' recognises both historical continuity and change. On the one hand, it acknowledges that the

material realities and modes of representation established through colonialism are still very much with us today, even if the political map of the world has altered through decolonisation. But on the other hand, it prizes the promise, the possibility, and the continuing necessity of change, while recognising that important challenges and changes have already been achieved.[6]

Some time ago, I argued that post-communism is a complex phenomenon.[7] Though some sociologists of Eastern Europe have insisted that this period was formally over as soon as the countries that were either occupied by the Soviet Union or incorporated in the Soviet bloc joined the European Union,[8] I would be inclined to claim that the duration of post-communism and/or postcolonialism can be hardly determined by formal factors alone. It is not only a colonial state that a subjugated society endures but also a state of mind that continues long after the (re)establishment of formal independence or joining any structures of Western liberal democracy. The prose writings of Ričardas Gavelis and Romualdas Lankauskas seem to support this statement, even if they contain no formal discussions of either phenomenon. Most characters of Herkus Kunčius' novels are deeply embedded in the past, and the new identities they have acquired after the collapse of the previous regime are often nothing but masks put on in order to adapt to a new social and political system. In some cases, the masks stick so tightly to the characters that wear them as to suggest a new identity.

Kunčius explores the issues of masks and identities in many novels, especially *Geležinė Stalino pirštinė* (Stalin's Iron Glove) and *Kolūkio metraščiai* (Annals of the Collective Farm). Both novels have certain similarities as well as significant differences. The first one provides a fictional though well-researched account of the ascent to power of Nikolai Yezhov (the head of the NKVD) and his eventual downfall, while *Annals of the Collective Farm* is a narrative about how collective farms were created in Soviet Lithuania after it was occupied and colonized by the Soviet Union. The protagonist of the former is a real historical person, and Vytautas – the protagonist of the latter – is the fictional chairman of a *kolkhoz* (Soviet collective farm).

Stalin's Iron Glove covers the period during which Soviet power came into being in Russia and its neighboring countries due to the spell of the communist vision disseminated by would-be politicians and appreciated by some layers of society. The plot is relatively simple: it follows the rise and fall of the head of the NKVD (Soviet secret service), who was born in the territory of Lithuania before finding himself in Moscow among the closest and most willing helpers and, eventually, executioners of Joseph Stalin. Being a dwarf by birth, Yezhov abandons his humble environment to become one of the most horrible supervisors of the NKVD before eventually becoming a victim of this infamous institution. Together with his senior fellows, he designed the Gulags for those who refused to submit to progress and the Communist Party of the Soviet Union, which claimed to be the 'locomotive of social progress.'

Kunčius provides a description of a Gulag viewed from the eyes of its designers. As the narrator explains,

> Tens and later hundreds of thousands of enemies of the people could admire the nature of the North, enjoy the cool weather throughout the year, and in their free time from the construction of the Belomorkanal, if they could still drag their feet, develop their hidden talents and fully educate themselves. In the Solovki prison camp, an excellent library has been operating since the time of Vladimir Lenin, a prisoners' theater and a circus were established here, and a brass band rehearsed. Enemies of the people who did not have time to die from slave labor and hunger, with the approval of the head of the camp, Fyodor Ivanovich Eikhmans [Teodors Eihmans], and the liberal leadership, organized reading contests among the barbarians, where every prisoner who had memorized the Short Course of the VKPb could appear on stage.[9]

The description is, of course, a satire of the experience that was painful, brutal, and often fatal. However, Kunčius makes the unspeakable speakable while using his favorite (occasionally perhaps somewhat repetitive) repertoire of literary devices. Adapting a mixture of Soviet newspeak and its categories, the writer produces a text mimicking the style of Soviet media reports. To some who have first-hand experience of the Soviet reality, this, quite possibly, evokes memories of the era; for readers of other generations or, for that matter, individuals who were born into different social realities, this might be more difficult to comprehend adequately.

Closely narrating Yezhov's ascent to power, Kunčius demonstrates how the Soviet system of repression worked and how the most ordinary individuals with no education and devoid of any gifts could ascend to power. Yezhov – a modest Pole from the colonial city of Wilno (Vilnius) with hardly any chance of forging a career due to the collapse of the old bourgeois system – sees his chance to climb the ladders of power until he becomes a member of a small group at the top of the Soviet authorities.

Running a powerful secret police empire, he is above everyone else in the hierarchy and is alongside only Stalin until everything collapses. He learns that there is only one individual in the new power system who can determine the destinies of even his closest and most loyal subordinates. Yezhov's house of cards is destroyed, and, ironically, his death sentence is carried out by the same person to whom he previously gave orders to kill "enemies of the state" for a number of years. It implies that some executioners don't outlive their victims...

When reading the novel, however, one cannot help but feel that this autopsy of the Soviet totalitarian system is long overdue. The events described belong to a distant past; in a certain sense, it is a historical novel rather than a dissection of power mechanisms that continue to exist. Nevertheless, viewed from the perspective of recent events, especially Russia's war against Ukraine and attempts to rehabilitate practices of Stalin's regime, the novel has some undeniable relevance, and its narrative is more than another entry to the 'illustrated history' genre. Kunčius' novel is simultaneously a well-researched and detailed yet fictional story of the rise and fall of a notorious Soviet figure told through the application of sarcasm, grotesque, and considerable black humor, as well as a literary introduction to certain horrific periods of Soviet history when a human being was just a small cog in the hands of the powerful. On the other hand, however, the narrative can be viewed as a fictionalized collection of the absurdities, contradictions, and paradoxes of the whole Soviet system, which, fortunately, had already disintegrated despite Moscow's desperate efforts to resuscitate it after the spectacular demise of the Soviet Union.

Enduring Power and Shifting Identities

Annals of the Collective Farm provides a short history of how collective farms were introduced in Sovietized Lithuania. Vytautas – a young man in his late twenties – is appointed the chairman of a *kolkhoz* and is responsible for establishing one in his vicinity. Using the narrative style typical of the Soviet press, Kunčius tells the story of how this young man, seduced by the promise of power, slowly progresses, taking an active part in recreating his society. Like in most of his prose writings, Kunčius employs irony and grotesqueness together with a large amount of (mostly) black humor. Sometimes, these literary devices are used so excessively that the whole narrative becomes somewhat monotonous and repetitive. Nevertheless, his ability to use the style of the Soviet press as well as Soviet history textbooks is remarkable. For example, he described the creation of Soviet power in Lithuania with a dose of grotesque as follows. Semionas Duškinas, the local head of the Communist Party, befriends Vytautas and briefly outlines to him why Soviet power was destined to be imported to an 'underdeveloped' independent (bourgeois) country:

> After the second glass of moonshine, his friend Duškinas began to tell the chairman of the collective farm how life was in bourgeois Lithuania. A pitiful picture opened before his eyes.

The beastly repression, the pathological oppression of the working people before the restoration of Soviet power in Lithuania, appears to have reached an appalling scale. There were wails, moans, and cries for help from all sides. Everywhere you looked, religious superstitions were rampant, bonfires were burning. The bourgeoisie, supported by the priests, kept the labor leader in the dark on a short leash. Cities and towns were drowning in mud. The village was starving. Everyone was walking barefoot with bloody heels, blistered palms; they hadn't washed in years, they hadn't seen soap, they were scarred. You wouldn't have found education even with a light. Folk culture was languishing. The same can be said about the agricultural situation, finances, and public transport. Therefore, it is natural, Duškinas taught the chairman of the collective farm, that conscious working people began to look at the USSR – the most advanced country in the world, where everything is abundant.

And the people of the great country, being sensitive to the pain of others, could not look on indifferently when such horrors were happening on their side.[10]

The novel provides an account of how Vytautas, the chairman of the *kolkhoz*, rises from a pro-communist teenager to the rank of an important Soviet bureaucrat who runs the collective farm and participates takes part in establishing the system of these farms in Soviet Lithuania. Vytautas' career constitutes the fabula of the novel, and the reader follows the progress of this humble teenager to an almighty Soviet bureaucrat who has a huge influence on the lives of the people working on his collective farm.

The whole novel might be regarded as a satire, as each and every episode relating to Soviet history is presented with the utmost irony. Kunčius uses Vytautas to show the peculiarities of Soviet life; each chapter brings him into a different historical situation and a different geographic location: Vytautas finds himself in various parts of the Soviet Union, including Moscow. Among many other places he visits, the chairman goes to Moscow to take part in the International Festival of Youth and Students, where he gets acquainted with a KGB officer named Sergey and a Congolese anti-colonialist movement leader called Patrice Lumumba. However, all these encounters are presented with the utmost grotesque typical of Kunčius' narratives. For example, Patrice spends most of his time with Russian girls, consumes a lot of alcohol, and behaves in a strange way. Eventually, he and his friends are captured by Moscow police before Sergey comes to their rescue.

Though most of these stories are basically nonsensical, they are used to create an absurd atmosphere of official Soviet life that differed significantly from private life in the state. The author seems to imply that every event in the Soviet realm was more or less a piece of nonsense. Of course, Soviet life balanced on the border of the absurd, and often this border was transgressed. The newspeak developed by the designers of the Soviet system often masqued this inherent absurdity of the regime and the life it generated. For example, the norms of morality were socially engineered by the system's designers. The people, including members of the Communist Party, were indoctrinated according to these socially engineered norms. Criminal acts committed by the regime's highest officials were interpreted by loyal party members as vices. Kunčius scoffs at such an inversion of values by providing a narrative about how Vytautas reacts to the news of new official policy consolidated by Yuri Andropov, who became the new paramount leader of the Soviet Union following the death of Leonid Brezhnev. After hearing the good news, Vytautas succumbs to the flow of memory:

> And indeed, life was simpler back then. No one was in doubt as to where was black and where was white. Or who is a good person and who is a bad person. There was less paperwork and bureaucratic procedures. If a scoundrel had to be shot, there was no need to rush to the prosecutor or ask for the mercy of the court to pronounce a sentence on the bad guy. That is why the work in the collective farm went faster then, Vytautas was convinced. No matter how you looked at it, under the rule of Comrade Stalin, Lithuania turned from a hopelessly backward agricultural country into an industrialized republic in a few years: heavy and light industry flourished, and culture reached unprecedented heights. Now, unfortunately, everything has stagnated, people's enthusiasm has faded. But Comrade Andropov will bring order, the country will move back from the brink of death.[11]

However, the degradation and final collapse of the Soviet Union had consequences for the people who ran the *kolkhozes*, including Vytautas, who, after the failure of the Moscow putsch, realized he had to join a national organization. Accordingly, he becomes a member of a popular pagan movement in order to survive and thrive. This happens after learning about the failed putsch in Moscow, which ends his illusion that the Soviet power might get Lithuania – now independent – back. The notorious *kolkhoz* chairman realized the implications of these developments and, like some other former communists, seized upon an opportunity to radically change his political and social views in order to secure at least some of his former power. Kunčius describes this transformation as a semi-religious experience that imitates one's conversion and initiation into a new group of believers:

> However, at that moment, when the chairman of the collective farm was already tying a noose around his neck, determined to hang himself from the

silo tower in protest, lightning suddenly flashed in the clear sky. Thunder
was heard. The sky opened up. And the God of Heaven appeared to the
chairman of the collective farm in his entire being. He did not appear alone
in the heights. Below, as if on waves in the firmament of the sky, was his
subordinate Potrimpo – the guardian of the earth; next to him, Perkūnas, the
ruler of the sky, as well as the mighty Peckols – the king of the underworld.
The ancient Lithuanian pagan gods looked down on the communist. He was
silent for a while, then he began to speak.[12]

After this miraculous conversion, Vytautas becomes an ardent pagan,
shaking off the troublesome shadows of the past and setting his eyes on the
early Baltic pagan culture as an escape from his past. As a newly-born
pagan, he begins to worship new gods, including those he refused to
acknowledge in previous phases of his life while he was a staunch
communist. Most importantly, this change of 'religious' attitudes secures
him a leading position in post-Soviet society, where he continues to have a
leading role. Though his social roles change, he manages to maintain his
power. Thus, the essential features of colonialism continue to exist in a
postcolonial society as individuals like Vytautas remain in charge. Despite
its (black) humor, irony, and sarcasm, the narrative poses uncomfortable
questions: Will this kind of ambiguity continue? If so, for how long? It
seems, however, that the writer himself has no answers.

   While constructing the narrative of his novel, Kunčius follows the path
Robert Zemeckis (coincidentally a director and producer with Lithuanian
roots) took in *Forrest Gump*. Like Zemeckis, Kunčius uses his protagonist
Vytautas to serve as a figure that allows him to tell the whole story of
Lithuania's occupation and Sovietization, bringing the reader to the collapse
of the regime and the tumultuous post-Soviet reality. This narrative strategy
contains certain advantages, as the author can choose the most curious,
juicy, or controversial episodes from the past. Yet as a piece of social
critique, his narrative is less impressive, especially since many events
described in the book relate to a distant past that poses almost no danger.
Nevertheless, Kunčius is conscious of issues concerning personal and
collective memory. There are several mnemonic groups in postcolonial
Lithuania that adhere to and develop contesting narratives about the past.
Some of them want to see the Soviet period as a 'natural' part of Lithuania's
history and therefore consider certain leaders from the Soviet period as
historical figures who were always loyal to their nation and culture,
suggesting that they chose the communist ideology and positions in a
colonial government as a kind of cover for the work they did for the good
of their homeland.

Notes

[1] Kunčius, *Pijoko chrestomatija*, 36.

[2] The term 'the Land of Mary' is regularly used in Kunčius' novel. The phrase refers to a real event when the mayor of Vilnius Region, Marija Rekst, announced that the region had been given over to the protection of the Virgin Mary. The author modestly omits that almost the same procedure was performed by the chairman of the Lithuanian parliament, Vytautas Landsbergis, who donated all of Lithuania to the Virgin Mary's care during the period of political transformations. These were curious episodes when politics and religion were merged by certain nationalist politicians.

[3] Kunčius, *Pijoko chrestomatija*, 48.

[4] Ibid, 49.

[5] Kelertas, *Kita vertus*, 230.

[6] McLeod, *Beginning Postcolonialism*, 33.

[7] Samalavičius, "An Amorphous Society."

[8] Samalavičius, "Ideology Never Ends."

[9] Kunčius, *Geležinė Stalino pirštinė*, 255.

[10] Kunčius, *Kolūkio metraščiai*, 21–22.

[11] Ibid, 194.

[12] Ibid, 243–244.

Works Cited

Kelertas, Violeta. *Kita vertus: straipsniai apie lietuvių literatūrą*. Vilnius: Baltos lankos, 2006.

Kunčius, Herkus. *Geležinė Stalino pirštinė*, Vilnius: LRS leidykla, 2020.

—. *Kolūkio metraščiai*. Vilnius: LRS leidykla, 2021.

—. *Pijoko chrestomatija*. Vilnius: Versus aureus, 2009.

McLeod, John. *Beginning Postcolonialism*. Manchester: Manchester University Press, 2000.

Samalavičius, Almantas. "An Amorphous Society: Lithuania in the Era of High Post-Communism." *Eurozine*, June 11, 2008. https://www.eurozine.com/an-amorphous-society/.

Samalavičius, Almantas. "Ideology Never Ends: An Interview with Sociologist Daniel Chirot." *Eurozine*, May 22, 2012. https://www.eurozine.com/ideology-never-ends/.

AFTERWORD

LITHUANIAN POSTCOLONIALISM AND BEYOND

In 1990, Lithuania said a firm (and hopefully final and irreversible) farewell to the colonial communist regime and its avatars. It is well-known that Lithuania was the first of the three occupied and eventually colonized Baltic states to break with the Soviet Union. The period between its miraculous escape and its acceptance into the European Union and, sometime later, NATO is generally referred to as post-communism or post-socialism. Curiously, these terms were not often used in the official discourse after the collapse of the colonial regime. Politicians generally avoided the terms, which were not much debated in the intellectual and academic milieu either. Intellectuals and academics were reluctant to use the terms and showed little interest in analyzing and discussing the contents of these important descriptive categories. The same applies to the notion of postcolonialism, which was excluded from the vocabulary of Lithuanian writers, intellectuals, and academics for quite a long time, as if it was meant exclusively for African or Asian countries.

This curious tendency to avoid certain conceptual terms became especially visible after Lithuania, as well as other Baltic and Eastern European states, joined the European Union. Many scholars took this fact as an opportunity to discontinue discussions about the specificity of Lithuanian (and Baltic) post-communism or postcolonialism. On the other hand, categories like post-communism, post-socialism, and the like had a currency in Western countries, or what is today known as the Northern Hemisphere. Dozens or even perhaps hundreds of books analyzing the former Soviet or Soviet-dominated space were written during the post-communist era. With a certain delay, these categories were accepted in local discourse. However, as soon as Lithuania and other Baltic states entered the European Union, they were immediately discarded.

Unlike post-communism, postcolonialism remained outside the borders of intellectual and academic discourse in Lithuania. The situation in the other Baltic countries (Latvia and Estonia) is somewhat better as researchers have long since discovered the potential of postcolonial critique and questioned aspects of its applicability to Baltic studies. Curiously, almost two decades since postcolonialism was introduced to Lithuanian academic and public discourses, it is still largely ignored in the social sciences and humanities, except for the fields of literary scholarship, theater, art, and film studies. Lithuanian writers and public intellectuals are still inclined to bypass this 'exotic' discipline.

The process of adopting postcolonialism for analyzing Baltic cultures and societies was reluctant and slow. Many local scholars, intellectuals, and cultural critics were convinced that postcolonialism solely applies to parts of Africa and Asia; thus, attempts to incorporate its framework for the analysis of post-Soviet cultures were usually rejected without much explanation. Recently, the situation has started to change to a certain degree; nevertheless, Lithuanian scholars are still reluctant to apply the framework of postcolonial studies to their society. Moreover, there are almost no discussions as to which elements of postcolonial theory are applicable and which need to be rejected or revised.

Last but not least, Lithuanian researchers do not enter into discussions of the postcolonial framework with colleagues in other postcolonial societies, even those that are not that distant (e.g., Ireland). So far, there have been almost no joint Baltic research or conference projects on Eastern European or Baltic postcolonialism in Lithuania, except for a very small number of conference sections and journal articles.

After decades of reluctance, the situation is finally changing, and quite a few young researchers have attempted to make use of postcolonial studies. So far, fewer attempts have been made to re-examine postcolonialism as a discourse and to discuss its limits and shortcomings. Most likely, this will happen in the future when Baltic studies scholars reach this methodology's glass ceiling. For now, however, there are still many things to be done before this happens. Of course, some aspects of postcolonial studies can hardly be applied to the Baltic or Eastern European domain as they have been developed to fit the analysis of 'classical colonialism.' But even these difficulties should not prevent the application of postcolonial studies to Baltic cultures and societies as they provide a valuable set of approaches and methods of study.

Though more than three decades have passed since the Baltic states freed themselves from the colonial regime that simultaneously preached to the West about the atrocities of the latter's colonial policies, each Baltic society currently faces its own socio-political and cultural issues. Only a few Lithuanian writers like Ričardas Gavelis have presented timely critiques of the post-communist/postcolonial society and its transformations. Most of his fellow writers were and continue to be reluctant to follow in his footsteps, choosing safer and more convenient strategies that withhold from social and cultural criticism by keeping silent and avoiding political issues or even accommodating the interests of the ruling power by staying away from the most serious and often controversial problems.

Many intellectuals, including writers, betrayed their societies in the past when the Soviet Union set out to occupy and eventually colonize their home countries in 1940 and toward the end of World War II. Some writers, intellectuals, and academics emigrated before the approaching Red Army seized control of the borders, allowing no one to leave. Many who stayed in the country soon became voluntary or involuntary supporters of the Soviet regime and sang songs worshipping Joseph Stalin, the Communist Party of the Soviet Union, and the new 'people's government.' Some writers even joined the ranks of the NKVD, KGB, and other power structures. Of course, despite being loyal to the new regime, many writers tried to preserve elements of their self-respect and refused to stop writing instead of putting their writings to the service or manipulations of the regime. The majority, however, chose to be co-opted by the authorities, joined the ranks of the Communist Party, and collaborated with those in power. After the re-establishment of Lithuania's independence and the failed Soviet putsch, many of them had a lot of excuses for previously collaborating with the Soviet regime and willingly or unwillingly performing the roles of 'engineers of the souls' under the orders and guidelines coming from the colonial center.

Alas, while the Soviet colonial regime collapsed more than three decades ago, the habits of thinking and acting under colonial power have largely persisted, even if they have often taken on new, less visible, and more sophisticated forms. Unfortunately, in postcolonial Lithuanian culture, there are very few writers who make conscious attempts to unwrap the mechanisms of often ambiguous transformations and question the shifting identities, masks, and roles of postcolonial individuals as well as their communities. It is hardly surprising that Lithuanian writers are more eager to revisit the past than to try to unwrap the issues that burden the present society and its individuals. The Soviet period is usually viewed as a strange, exotic, and totally detached historical period that has almost no relation to the present reality; it is often described as a world that has died and will remain dead. Needless to say, this raises concerns. If literature is blind and deaf to the continuity of the past in the present, it bypasses some very uncomfortable issues and abandons its role of reflecting upon society in the form of fictional narratives.

This book has presented both an overview and analysis of some tendencies in Lithuanian literature (and culture) in relation to socio-political and cultural developments that followed the fall of the Soviet regime in the

Baltics. Nevertheless, colonialism and postcolonialism in the region need to be further discussed as many of their aspects have not yet been adequately addressed. Hopefully, this book will provide some impetus for further reflections on the subject matter and, perhaps, trigger more inquiries into the region's contemporary postcolonial society that is slowly and gradually reconstructing itself. What will come out of this slow process in the near future can hardly be forecast. More than three decades since the colonial regime finally collapsed in the Baltics, society is still facing numerous problems and challenges. Curiously, Russia's war against Ukraine has largely been used by Lithuanian politicians as an excuse to address pressing issues at home and bypass a lot of important issues.

For better or worse, the naïve optimism of the transition period is over. These days, society is somewhat more mature and experienced, albeit also more exhausted, no less vulnerable to manipulations, and often dangerously divided over political, economic and cultural issues. Despite having a lengthy (and valuable) experience of living in a society of total control in which relations of dominance and submission were firmly established and, at the same time, cunningly disguised, many postcolonial writers and intellectuals remained morally short-sighted, believing that the burden of the past disappeared forever as soon as their country escaped the web of Soviet colonialism. The very fact that there are few, if any, fiction writers who are eager and ready to step into the shoes of their remarkably insightful and morally committed predecessors like Ričardas Gavelis makes one feel uneasy. The obvious, undisputable lack of fictional narratives of this magnitude into the mechanisms of power, manipulation, and control during the Soviet period, as well as into their present, far more sophisticated forms, is in many ways unsettling. Most likely, one should not expect writers to become sociologists of their respective society, but ambitious and high-quality fiction often gives an impulse to the sociological imagination.

There is no doubt, however, that postcolonial societies in the Baltic region and beyond are still facing many challenges even decades after the fall of the respective colonial regimes. The application of postcolonial theory to the study of literature and culture is, of course, neither a guarantee of any future immunity to society's social or political ills nor any panacea in cultural terms. However, this kind of inquiry could, perhaps, contribute to a better and more adequate understanding of society's past and present, its achievements and its failures.